Sustainable marketing has moved from the margins to the center of modern business strategy. Today's consumers expect brands to act responsibly, communicate transparently, and contribute meaningfully to society. This book is written for marketers, leaders, and founders who understand that sustainability is no longer a choice, but a requirement for long-term relevance and trust.

The book explores the rise of the conscious consumer and explains how changing values, digital transparency, and global awareness are reshaping buying behavior. It clarifies what sustainability truly means in a marketing context, separating authentic impact from superficial claims, and showing how responsible practices directly influence brand credibility and loyalty.

Moving from insight to action, the book outlines how organizations can build purpose-driven brands, design sustainable products, and communicate ethically without greenwashing. It also examines the role of digital marketing, data, partnerships, and measurement in creating scalable and accountable sustainability strategies.

Throughout the chapters, readers are guided through practical frameworks, strategic questions, and real-world scenarios that help translate sustainability principles into everyday marketing decisions. The focus remains on integration—ensuring sustainability is embedded into strategy, operations, and culture rather than treated as a standalone initiative.

Finally, the book looks ahead to the future of sustainable marketing, offering practical lessons, real-world examples, and a forward-looking perspective on how brands can win in a conscious consumer world through consistency, credibility, and long-term vision.

For permission requests, contact the author at:
contact@divyamagarwal.com

This book is self-published by the author.


ISBN: 978-93-342-9672-3
First Edition: May 2025

Printed in India

# Sustainable Marketing

**(Winning in a Conscious Consumer World)**

Thank you for choosing *Sustainable Marketing: Winning in a Conscious Consumer World*. By picking up this book, you have taken a deliberate step toward understanding how marketing can create value not only for businesses, but also for society and the planet. Your interest reflects a commitment to thoughtful leadership, responsible decision-making, and long-term impact. It is my hope that the ideas, frameworks, and perspectives in these pages support you in building brands that earn trust, drive meaningful growth, and contribute positively to a more sustainable future.

# Table of Contents

# The Rise of the Conscious Consumer

# Evolution of Consumer Values in the 21st Century

The evolution of consumer values in the 21st century represents one of the most profound shifts in modern market history. Unlike previous eras, where consumption was largely driven by availability, price, and functional utility, today's consumers operate within a far more complex value system. This transformation has been shaped by globalization, digital connectivity, environmental awareness, social movements, and a growing skepticism toward traditional corporate narratives. As a result, consumer decision-making has expanded beyond individual needs to include broader ethical, social, and environmental considerations.

At the beginning of the 21st century, consumption was still heavily influenced by economic growth narratives inherited from the late 20th century. Success was closely associated with material acquisition, brand status, and convenience. Brands competed aggressively on scale, efficiency, and aspirational messaging, often prioritizing speed to market and cost reduction above all else. During this phase, consumers largely accepted corporate claims at face value, with limited access to independent information or alternative viewpoints. Trust in institutions, media, and major brands was relatively high, and scrutiny of supply chains or labor practices remained minimal.

However, this dynamic began to shift rapidly with the expansion of the internet and, later, social media platforms. Information asymmetry between companies and consumers started to collapse. Consumers gained unprecedented access to product reviews, investigative journalism, activist content, and peer-to-peer discussions. This transparency fundamentally altered power dynamics, enabling individuals to question marketing claims, expose unethical practices, and mobilize collective action. As visibility increased, so did accountability, marking the early stages of value-driven consumption.

Environmental awareness emerged as a critical catalyst in reshaping consumer values. Climate change, pollution, biodiversity loss, and resource depletion moved from abstract scientific discussions to tangible realities affecting daily life. Extreme weather events, water scarcity, and declining air quality made environmental issues personal rather than theoretical. Consumers began to recognize the link between their purchasing choices and broader ecological outcomes. This awareness gradually shifted preferences toward products and brands perceived as environmentally responsible, energy-efficient, recyclable, or low-impact.

Simultaneously, social values gained prominence as consumers became more attuned to issues of inequality, labor rights, diversity, and inclusion. Global supply chains exposed stark contrasts between consumption in developed markets and production conditions in developing regions. Reports of unsafe working environments, child labor, and unfair wages triggered moral questioning among consumers. Purchasing decisions increasingly became expressions of personal values, with consumers using their spending power to support or reject companies based on perceived ethical alignment.

The rise of millennial and Gen Z consumers accelerated this transformation. These generations grew up in a digitally connected world marked by economic uncertainty, climate anxiety, and social activism. Unlike earlier generations, they demonstrated a willingness to challenge traditional corporate authority and demand authenticity. For them, brands were no longer distant entities but participants in cultural and social conversations. Values such as transparency, fairness, inclusivity, and sustainability became baseline expectations rather than differentiators.

Trust, once assumed, became conditional. Consumers began to expect brands to substantiate their claims with evidence, data, and consistent behavior over time. Vague sustainability slogans or purpose statements without action were increasingly viewed with suspicion. This skepticism gave rise to the concept of "earned trust," where credibility is built through demonstrated commitment rather than marketing rhetoric. Brands that failed to meet these expectations faced public backlash, boycotts, and reputational damage amplified by social media.

Another defining shift in consumer values has been the growing emphasis on long-term impact over short-term gratification. While convenience and price remain important, many consumers now balance these factors against durability, quality, and lifecycle impact. Concepts such as minimalism, conscious consumption, and circular economy thinking gained traction, encouraging consumers to buy less, buy better, and consider reuse or resale. This shift challenged the traditional growth model based on volume-driven consumption and frequent replacement.

Health and well-being also emerged as central consumer values, particularly in response to rising lifestyle-related illnesses and global health crises. Consumers became more attentive to ingredients, sourcing, and production methods, linking personal health with environmental and social sustainability. This holistic view reframed consumption as an extension of self-care and responsibility, further deepening the emotional dimension of purchasing decisions.

Cultural awareness and identity have also played a significant role in shaping modern consumer values. Globalization exposed consumers to diverse perspectives, traditions, and social norms, fostering sensitivity to cultural representation and appropriation. Consumers increasingly expect brands to respect local contexts, avoid stereotypes, and contribute positively to communities. Marketing missteps that ignore cultural nuances are quickly identified and criticized, reinforcing the importance of inclusivity and respect in brand communication.

Economic disruptions, including financial crises and rising inequality, have further influenced consumer priorities. Periods of instability encouraged skepticism toward unchecked corporate growth and profit maximization. Many consumers began to question who truly benefits from economic systems and demanded greater corporate responsibility in addressing societal challenges. This shift reframed consumption as a political and ethical act, not merely a personal one.

Technology has continued to shape values by enabling personalization, convenience, and immediacy, while simultaneously raising concerns around privacy, data usage, and digital well-being. Consumers appreciate innovation but increasingly expect ethical boundaries in how their data is collected and used. This dual expectation reflects a broader pattern in 21st-century consumer values: a desire for progress balanced with responsibility and respect for individual rights.

Importantly, these evolving values are not uniform across all consumers or markets. Socioeconomic conditions, cultural contexts, and regional priorities continue to influence how sustainability and ethics are interpreted. However, the overarching trend is clear: value-based considerations are moving from the periphery to the core of consumer decision-making. Even consumers who do not actively seek sustainable products are increasingly influenced by norms established by more values-driven segments.

For marketers, this evolution represents both a challenge and an opportunity. Traditional persuasive techniques focused solely on aspiration or price are no longer sufficient. Consumers expect brands to demonstrate alignment between stated values and operational reality. This requires deeper integration of sustainability, ethics, and social responsibility into business models rather than superficial marketing adjustments.

The evolution of consumer values in the 21st century ultimately reflects a broader societal transition toward accountability, interconnectedness, and long-term thinking. Consumption is no longer viewed in isolation from its consequences. Instead, it is increasingly understood as a force that shapes environmental outcomes, social structures, and future generations. Brands that recognize and respect this shift are better positioned to build trust, loyalty, and relevance in a conscious consumer world.

As this evolution continues, consumer values will remain dynamic, influenced by emerging technologies, geopolitical developments, and environmental realities. What remains constant is the expectation that brands listen, adapt, and act responsibly. Understanding this evolution is not merely an academic exercise; it is foundational to designing marketing strategies that resonate authentically and endure in a rapidly changing global landscape.

## Sustainability as a Purchase Driver

Sustainability has evolved from a peripheral consideration into a meaningful purchase driver that actively shapes how consumers evaluate brands, products, and services. In the modern marketplace, purchasing decisions are no longer governed solely by price, convenience, or functionality. Instead, consumers increasingly assess whether a product aligns with their personal values, ethical beliefs, and long-term concerns about environmental and social impact. Sustainability, in this context, functions as both a rational and emotional motivator, influencing not just what people buy, but why they buy it.

At its core, sustainability as a purchase driver reflects a growing awareness of the consequences of consumption. Consumers are more conscious of how products are made, where materials come from, how workers are treated, and what happens to products at the end of their lifecycle. This awareness has been amplified by greater access to information, widespread media coverage of environmental crises, and public discourse around climate change and inequality. As a result, purchasing decisions increasingly carry moral weight, turning everyday transactions into expressions of responsibility and intent.

One of the key reasons sustainability influences purchasing behavior is the shift in perceived value. Traditionally, value was equated with affordability, durability, or brand prestige. Today, many consumers include ethical considerations within their definition of value. A sustainably produced product may be perceived as higher quality, safer, or more trustworthy, even if it carries a higher price. In this sense, sustainability adds an intangible dimension to value, enhancing brand credibility and emotional connection.

Trust plays a central role in making sustainability a decisive purchase factor. Consumers have grown skeptical of exaggerated claims and superficial branding, leading them to favor companies that demonstrate transparency and accountability. Certifications, third-party audits, traceable supply chains, and clear disclosures provide reassurance that sustainability claims are credible. When consumers trust a brand's commitment to sustainability, they are more likely to choose it repeatedly, recommend it to others, and remain loyal even when alternatives are cheaper or more accessible.

Emotional resonance is another powerful driver behind sustainable purchasing. Many consumers experience a sense of personal satisfaction or pride when choosing products that align with their values. This emotional reinforcement strengthens brand attachment and increases the likelihood of repeat purchases. Sustainability allows consumers to feel that they are contributing, even in small ways, to solving larger global challenges. This sense of participation transforms consumption from a passive activity into an active statement of identity.

The influence of sustainability on purchasing decisions is particularly strong among younger generations, who view ethical consumption as a norm rather than an exception. Millennials and Gen Z consumers often expect brands to take clear positions on environmental and social issues. For them, sustainability is not a bonus feature but a baseline requirement. Brands that fail to meet these expectations risk being perceived as outdated, irresponsible, or untrustworthy, regardless of product quality or pricing.

However, sustainability as a purchase driver is not limited to idealistic motivations. Practical considerations also play a role. Energy-efficient appliances reduce long-term costs, durable products offer better longevity, and responsibly sourced food is often associated with health benefits. In such cases, sustainability aligns with self-interest, reinforcing its influence on purchasing decisions. This convergence of ethical and economic incentives makes sustainability a particularly robust driver of consumer behavior.

Social influence further amplifies the role of sustainability in purchasing. Consumers are increasingly influenced by peer behavior, online communities, and public discourse. Sustainable choices are often shared on social media, discussed in reviews, and promoted through influencers and advocacy groups. As sustainable consumption becomes more visible, it shapes social norms and expectations, encouraging wider adoption. In this environment, choosing unsustainable options can carry social costs, while sustainable choices enhance social credibility.

Brand differentiation is another reason sustainability drives purchases. In crowded markets where functional differences between products are minimal, sustainability provides a meaningful point of distinction. Consumers often use sustainability as a heuristic to simplify decision-making, especially when comparing similar offerings. A brand with a clear and authentic sustainability narrative can stand out more effectively than one relying solely on traditional marketing claims.

Despite its growing importance, sustainability does not operate in isolation. It interacts with other purchase drivers such as price, quality, availability, and convenience. Most consumers engage in trade-offs, balancing their values with practical constraints. While few consumers make decisions based purely on sustainability, many factor it in as a deciding element when other attributes are comparable. This makes sustainability a powerful tie-breaker rather than a standalone determinant in many purchasing scenarios.

Price sensitivity remains a limiting factor for sustainable purchasing, particularly in markets with income constraints. However, as sustainable practices scale and costs decrease, the price gap between sustainable and conventional products continues to narrow. Consumers also demonstrate a willingness to pay a premium when sustainability benefits are clearly communicated and perceived as genuine. Transparency around why a product costs more often strengthens acceptance rather than resistance.

The credibility of sustainability messaging is critical in converting intent into purchase. Consumers are increasingly adept at identifying greenwashing and inconsistent behavior. When sustainability claims are vague, exaggerated, or disconnected from actual practices, they undermine trust and weaken purchase motivation. Conversely, specific, measurable, and verifiable claims strengthen confidence and reduce perceived risk in the buying decision.

Sustainability also influences post-purchase behavior, reinforcing its role as a long-term driver. Consumers who feel aligned with a brand's values are more forgiving of minor shortcomings, more likely to engage with the brand's content, and more open to trying new offerings. This extended relationship increases customer lifetime value and turns sustainability into a strategic asset rather than a short-term marketing lever.

From a psychological perspective, sustainable purchasing satisfies both intrinsic and extrinsic motivations. Intrinsically, it aligns with personal ethics and self-concept. Extrinsically, it offers social approval, brand trust, and perceived quality. This dual reinforcement makes sustainability particularly effective as a purchase driver, especially in categories where consumers are emotionally invested.

It is also important to recognize that sustainability expectations vary across regions and cultures. In some markets, environmental impact may dominate consumer concern, while in others, social responsibility or economic fairness may take precedence. Successful brands understand these nuances and adapt their sustainability narratives accordingly, ensuring relevance without compromising core values.

For businesses, the rise of sustainability as a purchase driver necessitates a shift in strategy. Sustainability cannot be treated as a marketing layer added after product development. It must be embedded into design, sourcing, operations, and communication. Only when sustainability is integrated across the value chain can it consistently influence purchasing decisions and withstand consumer scrutiny.

As global challenges intensify and awareness continues to grow, sustainability is likely to become an even stronger determinant of consumer choice. What is currently a competitive advantage will increasingly become a minimum requirement. Brands that recognize sustainability as a genuine purchase driver, rather than a trend, are better positioned to build trust, loyalty, and long-term relevance.

Ultimately, sustainability as a purchase driver reflects a deeper transformation in how consumers relate to brands and markets. Purchasing is no longer just about fulfilling needs; it is about aligning actions with values. Brands that respect this shift and respond with authenticity, transparency, and commitment will not only influence buying decisions but also contribute meaningfully to a more responsible and resilient economy.

## Trust, Transparency, and Ethical Expectations

Trust, transparency, and ethical expectations have become foundational pillars of the modern relationship between consumers and brands. In the 21st century, trust is no longer granted by default based on brand size, legacy, or market presence. Instead, it is earned continuously through consistent behavior, honest communication, and demonstrable responsibility. Consumers now approach brands with a heightened level of scrutiny, shaped by past corporate failures, public scandals, and widespread access to information. As a result, trust has evolved from a passive assumption into an active evaluation process embedded in every stage of the consumer journey.

Trust in today's marketplace is deeply interconnected with transparency. Consumers expect visibility into how products are made, how services are delivered, and how companies conduct themselves beyond marketing messages. This expectation extends across supply chains, labor practices, environmental impact, data usage, and corporate governance. Transparency is no longer perceived as a voluntary act of goodwill; it is viewed as a basic obligation. When brands withhold information, provide vague explanations, or appear evasive, consumers often interpret this as a signal that something is being hidden, eroding trust even in the absence of proven wrongdoing.

The demand for transparency has been amplified by digital technology and real-time communication. Social media, investigative journalism, consumer review platforms, and activist networks have reduced the distance between corporate actions and public awareness. A single incident can quickly become global news, and inconsistencies between stated values and actual behavior are rapidly exposed. In this environment, brands are not judged solely on their intentions but on their ability to withstand public scrutiny. Transparency acts as both a preventive measure and a credibility enhancer, allowing organizations to address issues openly rather than react defensively once trust has already been damaged.

Ethical expectations form the third critical component of this triad. Modern consumers increasingly expect brands to operate within a broader moral framework that considers societal and environmental consequences. Ethical behavior is no longer confined to legal compliance. While adherence to laws and regulations is essential, consumers often hold brands to higher standards than those mandated by policy. Issues such as fair labor practices, environmental stewardship, diversity and inclusion, responsible sourcing, and community impact are now central to how ethical performance is assessed.

These ethical expectations are shaped by shifting social norms and heightened awareness of global challenges. Climate change, inequality, data privacy concerns, and human rights issues have entered mainstream discourse, influencing how consumers perceive corporate responsibility. Brands are increasingly expected to acknowledge their role within these systems and take meaningful action rather than remain neutral. Silence or inaction on widely recognized issues can be interpreted as complicity, further raising the stakes for ethical engagement.

Trust is fundamentally built on consistency over time. Consumers evaluate whether a brand's actions align with its stated values across different contexts and situations. A company that promotes sustainability while engaging in environmentally harmful practices, or one that advocates inclusion while tolerating internal discrimination, risks severe credibility loss. Ethical expectations require coherence between messaging, operations, leadership behavior, and corporate culture. When alignment is present, trust deepens; when it is absent, skepticism intensifies.

Transparency also plays a critical role in managing imperfections. Consumers do not expect brands to be flawless, but they do expect honesty about challenges, limitations, and areas for improvement. Openly acknowledging shortcomings, outlining corrective actions, and reporting progress fosters credibility. This approach signals maturity and accountability, reinforcing trust even in difficult circumstances. In contrast, denial or deflection often magnifies reputational damage and invites further scrutiny.

The role of trust has expanded beyond individual transactions to encompass long-term relationships. Consumers are more likely to remain loyal to brands they trust, even when competitors offer lower prices or greater convenience. Trust reduces perceived risk, making consumers more comfortable trying new products, sharing personal data, or engaging with brand-led initiatives. In this sense, trust functions as an economic asset that directly influences customer lifetime value and brand resilience.

Data transparency has become a particularly sensitive area of ethical expectation. As digital marketing and personalization technologies advance, consumers are increasingly aware of how their data is collected, stored, and used. Ethical expectations now include respect for privacy, informed consent, and responsible data governance. Brands that misuse data or fail to protect it face not only regulatory consequences but also lasting trust erosion. Conversely, companies that clearly explain data practices and prioritize consumer control often strengthen their credibility and differentiation.

Ethical expectations also extend to leadership and governance. Consumers pay attention to who leads organizations, how decisions are made, and how accountability is enforced. Executive behavior, corporate lobbying, political involvement, and crisis responses all influence perceptions of ethical integrity. Trust can be undermined by leadership actions that contradict stated values, even if the brand's products remain unchanged. This highlights the interconnected nature of ethics, where brand reputation is shaped by the totality of organizational behavior.

Cultural and social sensitivity further influence trust and ethical expectations. In an increasingly globalized marketplace, consumers expect brands to respect local contexts, avoid exploitation, and engage responsibly with diverse communities. Marketing campaigns that ignore cultural nuances or reinforce stereotypes are quickly criticized, often resulting in public backlash. Ethical expectations now include an obligation to listen, learn, and adapt rather than impose uniform narratives across different markets.

The rise of ethical consumerism has also introduced a more participatory form of accountability. Consumers actively question brands, demand explanations, and organize collective responses through boycotts or advocacy campaigns. This shift reflects a broader rebalancing of power, where consumers see themselves as stakeholders rather than passive buyers. Trust is therefore co-created through ongoing dialogue rather than one-way communication.

From a strategic perspective, meeting trust, transparency, and ethical expectations requires systemic integration rather than isolated initiatives. These principles must be embedded into decision-making processes, performance metrics, and organizational incentives. Marketing teams alone cannot carry this responsibility; it requires cross-functional collaboration involving operations, supply chain management, human resources, legal teams, and leadership. When ethics and transparency are siloed, inconsistencies inevitably emerge.

Importantly, ethical expectations are not static. They evolve alongside societal values, technological developments, and global events. What was considered acceptable a decade ago may no longer meet contemporary standards. Brands must therefore engage in continuous learning and adaptation, monitoring shifts in public sentiment and regulatory landscapes. Trust is maintained not by rigid adherence to outdated practices, but by responsiveness and openness to change.

There is also a growing expectation for brands to contribute positively rather than merely minimize harm. Consumers increasingly value proactive initiatives that address social or environmental challenges in meaningful ways. This does not imply that every brand must become an activist organization, but it does suggest that ethical leadership involves taking responsibility for one's impact and leveraging influence constructively.

Failure to meet trust and ethical expectations carries significant consequences. Loss of consumer confidence can lead to declining sales, reputational damage, regulatory scrutiny, and difficulty attracting talent or investors. In contrast, brands that consistently demonstrate transparency and ethical integrity often benefit from stronger loyalty, advocacy, and long-term stability. Trust acts as a buffer during crises, allowing brands to recover more effectively when challenges arise.

In the context of sustainable marketing, trust, transparency, and ethical expectations are inseparable. Sustainability claims without transparency invite skepticism, while transparency without ethical substance offers little reassurance. Together, these elements form the foundation upon which credible sustainable marketing is built. They determine whether sustainability messaging is perceived as authentic commitment or opportunistic positioning.

Ultimately, the growing emphasis on trust, transparency, and ethics reflects a deeper shift in how consumers define responsible business. Brands are no longer evaluated solely on what they sell, but on how they operate and what they stand for. Trust has become a strategic currency, transparency a prerequisite for legitimacy, and ethics a defining measure of relevance. Organizations that understand and embrace these expectations are better equipped to build enduring relationships and succeed in a conscious consumer world.

# Generational Shifts: Gen Z and Millennial Influence

Generational shifts have played a decisive role in redefining consumer behavior in the 21st century, with Millennials and Gen Z emerging as the most influential forces shaping modern markets. These generations are not only significant in size and purchasing power but also distinct in their values, expectations, and relationship with brands. Their influence extends beyond their own consumption, setting new norms that increasingly affect older generations and forcing businesses to rethink traditional marketing models.

Millennials, broadly defined as those born between the early 1980s and mid-1990s, came of age during a period of rapid globalization, technological expansion, and economic disruption. They witnessed the rise of the internet, the 2008 global financial crisis, and growing awareness of climate change and social inequality. These experiences shaped a generation that is pragmatic, skeptical of institutions, and deeply aware of systemic challenges. As consumers, Millennials began to question unchecked corporate growth and demand greater accountability, laying the groundwork for values-driven consumption.

Gen Z, born from the mid-1990s onward, represents an even more pronounced shift. As digital natives, they have never known a world without smartphones, social media, or instant access to information. This constant connectivity has shaped their worldview, making them highly informed, socially aware, and accustomed to rapid feedback loops. Gen Z's expectations of brands are shaped not only by personal values but also by a culture of visibility, where actions are constantly observed, shared, and evaluated in public spaces.

One of the most significant contributions of Millennials and Gen Z is the normalization of values-based purchasing. For these generations, consumption is closely tied to identity and self-expression. They are more likely to support brands that align with their beliefs on sustainability, diversity, inclusion, and social justice. Purchasing decisions are often seen as extensions of personal ethics, turning brands into symbols of what consumers stand for rather than mere providers of goods or services.

Trust dynamics differ markedly for these generations compared to their predecessors. Millennials and Gen Z exhibit lower baseline trust in corporations, governments, and traditional advertising. This skepticism is rooted in repeated exposure to corporate scandals, misinformation, and perceived hypocrisy. As a result, trust must be earned through consistent action rather than polished messaging. Brands are expected to demonstrate authenticity, admit shortcomings, and engage in transparent dialogue rather than rely on aspirational narratives alone.

Both generations also expect brands to take responsibility beyond profit generation. Millennials were among the first to mainstream the idea that companies should have a purpose, while Gen Z has further raised expectations by demanding measurable impact. Purpose statements without tangible outcomes are quickly dismissed. These consumers look for evidence in the form of sustainability metrics, ethical sourcing practices, inclusive policies, and community engagement. In this context, purpose is not a branding exercise but a standard against which behavior is judged.

The influence of Millennials and Gen Z is particularly evident in their expectations around sustainability. Environmental consciousness is not viewed as a trend but as a necessity shaped by lived experience. Climate change, pollution, and resource scarcity are not abstract future threats for these generations; they are immediate realities. This has led to strong preferences for brands that demonstrate environmental responsibility through reduced emissions, sustainable materials, circular business models, and transparent reporting.

Social justice and inclusion are equally central to generational influence. Millennials and Gen Z expect brands to reflect diverse identities, challenge stereotypes, and contribute to equitable systems. Representation in advertising, inclusive product design, fair labor practices, and internal diversity are closely scrutinized. Brands that fail to meet these expectations risk being perceived as out of touch or exclusionary, regardless of product quality.

Digital behavior further amplifies generational impact. Millennials and Gen Z rely heavily on peer recommendations, online reviews, and social media communities when making purchasing decisions. Influencers, creators, and user-generated content often carry more credibility than traditional advertising. This shift has decentralized brand authority, placing greater power in the hands of consumers and communities. Brands are no longer the sole narrators of their story; they are participants in an ongoing conversation shaped by their audience.

Gen Z, in particular, has redefined expectations around speed and responsiveness. Accustomed to real-time communication, they expect brands to listen, respond, and adapt quickly. Silence or delayed responses during controversies are often interpreted as avoidance. This has increased pressure on organizations to align internal decision-making processes with the pace of digital discourse, ensuring that values are not only articulated but acted upon promptly.

Economic realities also shape generational influence. Millennials entered the workforce during periods of financial instability, while Gen Z faces rising living costs and uncertain job markets. These conditions have fostered a pragmatic approach to consumption. While values matter deeply, price and accessibility remain important considerations. As a result, these generations often seek brands that balance ethical commitments with affordability, rewarding companies that make sustainable and responsible options more accessible.

Importantly, Millennials and Gen Z are not passive consumers; they are active participants in shaping brand behavior. They engage in advocacy, call out inconsistencies, and mobilize collective action through digital platforms. Boycotts, viral campaigns, and public accountability efforts have become common tools for expressing dissatisfaction. This activism has redefined the consequences of misalignment between brand values and actions, increasing reputational risk for companies that fail to meet expectations.

Their influence also extends internally within organizations. As employees, Millennials and Gen Z expect workplaces to reflect the same values they seek as consumers. Employer branding, corporate culture, and internal ethics increasingly affect external brand perception. Companies that treat sustainability and ethics as marketing themes but neglect them internally often face credibility challenges as employees share experiences publicly.

The generational shift has also changed how loyalty is formed and maintained. Traditional loyalty driven by habit or lack of alternatives has given way to conditional loyalty based on alignment and performance. Millennials and Gen Z are willing to switch brands if values are compromised or better alternatives emerge. However, when alignment is strong, loyalty can be deep and advocacy-driven, with consumers actively promoting brands they believe in.

Despite their shared influence, it is important to recognize differences between Millennials and Gen Z. Millennials often balance idealism with practicality, shaped by responsibilities such as family and career stability. Gen Z tends to be more uncompromising in its expectations, reflecting both youth and heightened exposure to global challenges. Successful brands understand these nuances and tailor engagement strategies without diluting core values.

The influence of these generations has also accelerated broader market change. Practices once considered progressive, such as sustainability reporting or inclusive marketing, are increasingly becoming standard expectations. Even brands targeting older demographics are adopting values-driven strategies in response to norms set by Millennials and Gen Z. In this way, generational influence extends far beyond direct purchasing power.

For marketers, these shifts demand a fundamental change in approach. Messaging must be grounded in truth, supported by action, and open to scrutiny. Engagement must be dialogic rather than directive, recognizing consumers as informed stakeholders rather than passive recipients. Brands must be prepared to evolve continuously as generational values continue to develop.

Ultimately, the influence of Millennials and Gen Z represents a broader transformation in the relationship between business and society. These generations are redefining success not only in terms of personal achievement but also collective well-being. Their expectations challenge brands to operate with greater integrity, accountability, and foresight. Understanding and responding to these generational shifts is not simply a marketing requirement; it is essential to building relevance and resilience in a conscious consumer world.

## Cultural and Regional Variations in Conscious Consumption

Cultural and regional variations play a decisive role in shaping how conscious consumption is understood, prioritized, and practiced across global markets. While sustainability, ethics, and responsibility have emerged as broadly influential themes, they do not manifest uniformly across geographies. Consumer values are deeply embedded within cultural norms, economic realities, historical experiences, and social structures. As a result, what constitutes "conscious consumption" in one region may differ significantly in emphasis, motivation, and expression in another. Understanding these variations is essential for brands seeking to engage responsibly and authentically in diverse markets.

At its foundation, conscious consumption reflects how individuals interpret their responsibility toward society, the environment, and future generations. These interpretations are influenced by cultural beliefs about community, individualism, nature, and progress. In societies where collectivism is emphasized, consumption decisions are often evaluated based on their impact on family, community, or national well-being. In more individualistic cultures, conscious consumption may be framed as a personal ethical choice or an expression of individual identity. These underlying cultural orientations shape not only what consumers value, but how they expect brands to communicate and behave.

Economic context is one of the most significant factors driving regional differences in conscious consumption. In high-income markets, consumers generally have greater purchasing power and access to alternatives, allowing sustainability and ethics to play a more prominent role in decision-making. In these regions, conscious consumption often focuses on environmental impact, carbon reduction, animal welfare, and corporate transparency. Consumers may be willing to pay a premium for sustainable products, viewing such purchases as investments in long-term societal well-being.

In contrast, in emerging and developing markets, conscious consumption is often closely tied to affordability, accessibility, and immediate social impact. While environmental awareness is growing, priorities frequently center on issues such as fair pricing, job creation, health, and basic safety. Consumers in these regions may value brands that contribute to local economic development, provide stable employment, or improve access to essential goods. Conscious consumption here is less about symbolic ethical signaling and more about tangible improvements in quality of life.

Cultural attitudes toward nature also shape regional interpretations of sustainability. In some cultures, particularly those with strong indigenous or agrarian traditions, nature is viewed as something to be respected, preserved, and lived in harmony with. Conscious consumption in these contexts often emphasizes conservation, minimal waste, and respect for natural resources. In more industrialized societies, where separation from nature has historically been greater, sustainability may be framed as a corrective response to environmental damage rather than a continuation of existing values.

Historical experience further influences how consumers perceive corporate responsibility. Regions that have experienced exploitation, colonialism, or environmental degradation linked to industrial activity often exhibit heightened sensitivity to corporate behavior. In such contexts, consumers may be particularly skeptical of multinational brands and demand strong commitments to local sourcing, fair labor practices, and community investment. Conscious consumption becomes a means of reclaiming agency and ensuring that economic participation does not come at the cost of social or environmental harm.

Social norms and expectations also vary widely across regions, affecting how ethical consumption is practiced. In some cultures, public signaling of ethical choices is common and socially reinforced. Consumers may openly discuss sustainable brands, share ethical purchases on social media, and participate in collective actions such as boycotts. In other cultures, ethical behavior is considered a private matter, and overt moral signaling may be viewed with discomfort or suspicion. Brands must navigate these norms carefully to avoid appearing performative or culturally insensitive.

Religion and belief systems further shape conscious consumption patterns in many regions. Religious teachings often influence attitudes toward stewardship, fairness, waste, and community responsibility. In markets where religion plays a central role in daily life, ethical consumption may be guided by principles such as moderation, charity, or respect for life. Brands operating in these contexts must understand how sustainability and ethics intersect with spiritual values, ensuring alignment rather than contradiction.

Regional regulatory environments also affect consumer expectations and behavior. In markets with strong environmental and consumer protection laws, sustainability standards are often normalized and expected. Consumers may assume a baseline level of ethical behavior and focus their attention on brands that go beyond compliance. In regions with weaker regulatory frameworks, consumers may rely more heavily on brand reputation and informal trust networks to assess ethical performance. This shifts the burden of proof onto companies to demonstrate responsibility proactively.

Urbanization introduces another layer of variation. Urban consumers often have greater exposure to global trends, sustainability discourse, and ethical branding. They are more likely to encounter eco-friendly products, participate in digital activism, and engage with international narratives around climate and social justice. Rural consumers, while not less conscious, may prioritize local impact, durability, and practicality. Conscious consumption in rural contexts often manifests through support for local producers, resource efficiency, and long-term value rather than formal sustainability labels.

Education and access to information also influence how conscious consumption develops regionally. In markets where consumers have high levels of education and media access, awareness of complex sustainability issues tends to be greater. These consumers may scrutinize supply chains, certifications, and corporate disclosures in detail. In regions with limited access to information, conscious consumption may be driven more by trust, word-of-mouth, and visible outcomes rather than detailed metrics or reports. This does not imply lower ethical concern, but rather different mechanisms of evaluation.

Globalization has introduced both convergence and divergence in conscious consumption patterns. On one hand, global media, multinational brands, and digital platforms have spread shared narratives around sustainability, climate action, and social responsibility. On the other hand, local interpretations of these narratives remain deeply influenced by cultural context. A sustainability campaign that resonates strongly in one region may fail or even backfire in another if it conflicts with local values or realities.

Language and symbolism play a crucial role in how conscious consumption is communicated and understood. Concepts such as sustainability, ethics, or responsibility may not translate directly across cultures. Words carry different connotations, and symbols that signify care or progress in one culture may be interpreted differently elsewhere. Effective engagement requires careful adaptation of messaging to ensure that core values are communicated clearly without imposing external perspectives.

Regional differences are also evident in how consumers prioritize environmental versus social concerns. In some markets, climate change and environmental degradation dominate public discourse, making eco-friendly practices the primary focus of conscious consumption. In others, social issues such as labor rights, income inequality, or access to healthcare take precedence. Brands that treat sustainability as a one-dimensional concept risk overlooking these regional priorities and appearing disconnected from local realities.

The role of community varies significantly across cultures and directly influences consumption behavior. In tightly knit communities, purchasing decisions are often influenced by collective norms and shared expectations. Conscious consumption may be reinforced through communal practices, local initiatives, or social accountability. In more individualistic settings, consumers may act independently, guided by personal research and self-defined ethical standards. Brands must recognize whether influence operates primarily at the individual or community level within a given region.

Importantly, cultural and regional variations do not imply resistance to sustainability or ethical consumption. Rather, they highlight that conscious consumption is a contextual practice shaped by lived experience. Consumers across regions care deeply about fairness, well-being, and future security, but they express these concerns in ways that reflect their circumstances. Recognizing this diversity allows brands to engage more respectfully and effectively.

For global brands, these variations present both complexity and opportunity. Standardized sustainability strategies may ensure consistency, but without localization they risk irrelevance or misinterpretation. Conversely, excessive localization without a coherent ethical framework can dilute credibility. The challenge lies in maintaining core principles while adapting execution to local contexts. This requires deep cultural understanding, local partnerships, and ongoing dialogue with regional stakeholders.

Cultural sensitivity is particularly critical in marketing communication. Campaigns that adopt a moralizing tone or assume universal priorities can alienate consumers. Conscious consumption should be framed in ways that resonate with local values, whether through economic empowerment, community resilience, environmental preservation, or social equity. Authenticity emerges not from uniform messaging, but from relevance and respect.

As awareness of global challenges continues to grow, regional expressions of conscious consumption are likely to evolve. Economic development, education, and digital connectivity will influence how sustainability is prioritized and practiced. While differences will persist, the underlying expectation that brands act responsibly is becoming increasingly widespread. Conscious consumption is not a singular movement, but a mosaic of regional practices united by shared concern for impact.

Ultimately, understanding cultural and regional variations in conscious consumption is essential for building trust and relevance in a global marketplace. It requires moving beyond assumptions and engaging with consumers as participants in distinct social and cultural systems. Brands that listen, learn, and adapt are better positioned to contribute meaningfully while meeting diverse expectations.

In a conscious consumer world, success is not defined by imposing a single definition of responsibility, but by recognizing and honoring the many ways responsibility is understood and lived. Cultural and regional awareness transforms sustainability from a generic concept into a meaningful, locally grounded practice. This sensitivity not only strengthens brand relationships but also ensures that conscious consumption delivers real, context-specific value to the communities it aims to serve.

# Defining Sustainability in Marketing

## Environmental, Social, and Economic Pillars

The environmental, social, and economic pillars form the foundational framework of sustainability, often referred to as the "triple bottom line." Together, these pillars represent a holistic approach to responsible business and consumption, recognizing that long-term success cannot be achieved by focusing on profit alone. Instead, sustainable systems balance environmental protection, social well-being, and economic viability. In the context of modern marketing and business strategy, understanding these three interconnected pillars is essential to creating value that endures over time.

The environmental pillar addresses the impact of human activity on natural ecosystems and resources. It is rooted in the recognition that economic growth and consumption place significant strain on the planet's finite resources. Environmental sustainability focuses on minimizing harm to ecosystems while ensuring that natural systems remain capable of supporting future generations. This pillar encompasses issues such as climate change, biodiversity loss, pollution, water scarcity, and resource depletion, all of which have become increasingly visible and urgent in the 21st century.

At a business level, the environmental pillar involves evaluating how products are designed, manufactured, distributed, used, and disposed of. Lifecycle thinking is central to this approach, encouraging organizations to assess environmental impact from raw material extraction to end-of-life disposal. Reducing carbon emissions, improving energy efficiency, minimizing waste, and adopting renewable resources are key priorities. Environmental sustainability is no longer limited to compliance with regulations; it has become a strategic consideration that influences brand reputation, cost structures, and long-term resilience.

Consumers increasingly associate environmental responsibility with quality and credibility. Brands that demonstrate a genuine commitment to reducing environmental harm are often perceived as forward-thinking and trustworthy. However, environmental sustainability requires measurable action rather than symbolic gestures. Transparent reporting, science-based targets, and continuous improvement are critical to ensuring that environmental commitments translate into real-world impact.

The social pillar focuses on people, communities, and societal systems. It addresses how businesses affect employees, customers, suppliers, and the broader communities in which they operate. Social sustainability is concerned with equity, fairness, health, safety, and human dignity. It recognizes that economic activity should contribute positively to society rather than exacerbate inequality or exploitation.

Key aspects of the social pillar include fair labor practices, safe working conditions, diversity and inclusion, access to education and healthcare, and respect for human rights. In a globalized economy, social sustainability extends across complex supply chains, where conditions may vary significantly between regions. Businesses are increasingly expected to take responsibility for social impacts beyond their immediate operations, ensuring ethical standards are upheld throughout their value chain.

From a consumer perspective, social sustainability strongly influences trust and brand loyalty. Awareness of labor exploitation, discrimination, or community harm can quickly erode confidence in a brand. Conversely, companies that invest in employee well-being, support local communities, and promote inclusive practices often benefit from stronger engagement and advocacy. Social responsibility is not viewed as charity, but as an integral part of ethical business conduct.

The social pillar also encompasses how brands engage with cultural and societal issues. Representation, accessibility, and respectful communication have become important considerations, particularly in diverse and global markets. Consumers expect brands to reflect social realities thoughtfully and to avoid reinforcing harmful stereotypes. This expectation reinforces the need for organizations to embed social awareness into decision-making and marketing strategies.

The economic pillar focuses on financial viability, value creation, and long-term prosperity. Unlike traditional views that equate economic success solely with profit maximization, the sustainability framework emphasizes responsible and resilient economic growth. Economic sustainability ensures that businesses remain profitable and competitive while supporting stable employment, innovation, and economic inclusion.

A sustainable economic model prioritizes long-term value over short-term gains. This includes responsible investment, prudent risk management, and ethical governance. Businesses that neglect environmental or social considerations may achieve short-term profitability but expose themselves to regulatory penalties, reputational damage, and operational disruptions. Economic sustainability therefore depends on integrating environmental and social responsibility into core business strategy.

For consumers, economic sustainability influences perceptions of fairness and value. Pricing practices, accessibility, and affordability play a role in determining whether sustainability is inclusive or exclusive. Brands that balance ethical commitments with cost efficiency are better positioned to scale impact and reach broader audiences. Economic sustainability also involves supporting local economies, small suppliers, and innovation ecosystems that contribute to shared prosperity.

Importantly, the three pillars are deeply interconnected rather than independent. Environmental degradation often leads to social consequences, such as health risks or loss of livelihoods. Social inequality can undermine economic stability and growth. Economic pressures can, in turn, drive environmentally harmful practices if not managed responsibly. Sustainable systems recognize these interdependencies and seek solutions that address multiple dimensions simultaneously.

In practice, this interconnectedness means that trade-offs are sometimes unavoidable, but they must be managed thoughtfully. For example, transitioning to environmentally friendly materials may increase short-term costs but deliver long-term economic and social benefits. Similarly, investing in fair wages and safe working conditions can enhance productivity, reduce turnover, and strengthen brand reputation over time. Sustainable decision-making requires a long-term perspective that accounts for systemic impact.

From a marketing standpoint, the environmental, social, and economic pillars provide a framework for credible and coherent sustainability narratives. Brands that focus exclusively on one pillar risk appearing unbalanced or opportunistic. Environmental claims without social responsibility may overlook labor or community impact. Social initiatives without environmental consideration may ignore ecological harm. Economic success without ethical grounding increasingly lacks legitimacy in the eyes of conscious consumers.

Measurement and accountability are critical to maintaining balance across the three pillars. Clear metrics, targets, and reporting mechanisms help organizations track progress and identify gaps. This data-driven approach supports transparency and allows stakeholders to assess whether sustainability commitments are being met. Without measurement, sustainability risks becoming abstract or performative rather than operational.

Regulatory frameworks and global standards increasingly reflect the three-pillar model. ESG reporting, sustainability disclosures, and international guidelines emphasize environmental performance, social impact, and governance as integrated dimensions of responsible business. As these expectations become more standardized, organizations that already align with the three pillars are better prepared to adapt and comply.

Cultural and regional contexts influence how the pillars are prioritized. In some regions, environmental issues such as pollution or water scarcity may dominate sustainability discourse. In others, social concerns such as labor rights or economic inclusion may take precedence. However, long-term sustainability requires attention to all three pillars, even when emphasis varies by context.

For leaders and marketers, embracing the environmental, social, and economic pillars requires moving beyond isolated initiatives.

Sustainability must be embedded into strategy, operations, and communication. This integration ensures that commitments are consistent, credible, and resilient to scrutiny. When the pillars are aligned, sustainability becomes a source of innovation rather than a constraint.

Ultimately, the environmental, social, and economic pillars represent a shift in how success is defined. They challenge the notion that growth and responsibility are mutually exclusive, demonstrating instead that they are interdependent. Businesses that understand and operationalize this framework are better positioned to build trust, adapt to change, and contribute positively to society.

In a conscious consumer world, these pillars serve as both a compass and a benchmark. They guide decision-making, shape expectations, and provide a shared language for evaluating impact. By balancing environmental stewardship, social responsibility, and economic resilience, organizations can create value that extends beyond transactions and endures across generations.

## ESG, CSR, and Shared Value Explained

ESG, CSR, and Shared Value are three closely related but distinct frameworks that define how organizations understand and operationalize responsibility in the modern economy. While they are often used interchangeably in public discourse, each represents a different stage in the evolution of corporate responsibility and reflects a shift from peripheral ethical efforts to integrated, strategic value creation. Understanding the differences and connections between these concepts is essential for marketers, leaders, and decision-makers operating in a conscious consumer and investor-driven world.

Corporate Social Responsibility, commonly referred to as CSR, is the earliest and most traditional of the three frameworks. CSR emerged from the idea that businesses have obligations to society beyond generating profits. Historically, CSR focused on philanthropy, compliance, and reputation management. Companies engaged in charitable donations, community programs, employee volunteering, or environmental initiatives, often operating these efforts separately from core business activities. CSR was frequently treated as a goodwill exercise designed to demonstrate that a company was a responsible corporate citizen.

In many organizations, CSR functioned as a reactive or compensatory mechanism. Businesses would pursue profit-driven operations and later attempt to offset negative impacts through social initiatives. While CSR played an important role in raising awareness about corporate responsibility, it was often criticized for lacking accountability, measurement, and strategic integration. Because CSR initiatives were not always tied to business outcomes, they were vulnerable to budget cuts during economic downturns and sometimes perceived as superficial or performative.

Despite these limitations, CSR laid the groundwork for more structured approaches to responsibility. It normalized the idea that businesses should care about their impact on society and the environment. Over time, stakeholders began to demand greater transparency, consistency, and measurable outcomes from CSR activities. This pressure contributed directly to the emergence of ESG as a more rigorous and investor-oriented framework.

ESG, which stands for Environmental, Social, and Governance, represents a more formalized and data-driven approach to evaluating corporate performance. Unlike CSR, ESG is primarily used by investors, regulators, and financial institutions to assess risk, resilience, and long-term value. ESG focuses on how environmental practices, social responsibility, and governance structures affect a company's financial performance and sustainability over time. It shifts responsibility from being optional or reputational to being material and measurable.

The environmental component of ESG examines how a company manages its impact on the natural world. This includes emissions, energy use, waste management, resource efficiency, and climate risk exposure. The social component assesses how a company treats employees, customers, suppliers, and communities, including labor practices, diversity, human rights, and product responsibility. Governance focuses on leadership, ethics, transparency, board structure, executive compensation, and shareholder rights. Together, these factors provide a comprehensive view of how responsibly a company is managed.

One of the defining characteristics of ESG is its emphasis on metrics and disclosure. ESG performance is tracked through standardized indicators, ratings, and reports that allow stakeholders to compare companies across industries and regions. This emphasis on measurement addresses one of the key weaknesses of traditional CSR, making responsibility more accountable and less reliant on narrative alone. As ESG reporting becomes increasingly regulated, it has moved from a voluntary practice to a business necessity.

However, ESG is not without criticism. Some argue that ESG frameworks can become overly focused on compliance and box-ticking, prioritizing reporting over real impact. Others note inconsistencies in ESG ratings and methodologies, which can create confusion and skepticism. Despite these challenges, ESG has fundamentally changed how responsibility is perceived, embedding environmental and social considerations into financial decision-making and corporate governance.

Shared Value represents a more strategic and integrated evolution of corporate responsibility. Coined to describe the idea that businesses can create economic value in ways that also produce value for society, Shared Value moves beyond risk management and philanthropy. It reframes social and environmental challenges as opportunities for innovation, growth, and competitive advantage. Rather than asking how businesses can minimize harm, Shared Value asks how they can actively contribute to solving societal problems through their core operations.

Unlike CSR, which often exists alongside business strategy, Shared Value is embedded within it. Companies pursuing Shared Value redesign products, services, and business models to address unmet social needs while generating profit. This might involve developing affordable healthcare solutions, improving agricultural productivity through sustainable practices, or expanding access to financial services. In each case, societal benefit is not a byproduct but a central driver of economic success.

Shared Value also differs from ESG in its orientation. While ESG focuses on assessing and managing risk from an external perspective, Shared Value emphasizes opportunity creation from within the business. ESG asks whether a company is responsibly managed; Shared Value asks how responsibility can drive growth and differentiation. The two approaches are complementary rather than conflicting. Strong Shared Value strategies often improve ESG performance, while robust ESG governance supports sustainable value creation.

From a marketing perspective, these distinctions are critical. CSR-based messaging often highlights charitable initiatives or community involvement. ESG-aligned communication emphasizes transparency, accountability, and performance against recognized standards. Shared Value narratives focus on innovation, impact, and the alignment between business success and societal progress. Understanding which framework a brand is operating within helps ensure that messaging is credible and aligned with actual practices.

Consumers and stakeholders increasingly expect coherence across all three frameworks. CSR initiatives without ESG accountability may be viewed as superficial. ESG compliance without a Shared Value mindset may appear defensive or bureaucratic. Shared Value claims without evidence of governance and measurement risk skepticism. In a conscious consumer world, credibility is built when these approaches reinforce one another rather than operate in isolation.

The evolution from CSR to ESG to Shared Value also reflects changing expectations of corporate leadership. Businesses are no longer seen as passive participants in society but as powerful actors with the capacity to influence systemic outcomes. Stakeholders expect companies to acknowledge this influence and use it responsibly. This expectation applies not only to large multinationals but increasingly to mid-sized and emerging organizations as well.

Cultural and regional contexts influence how these frameworks are adopted and emphasized. In some markets, CSR remains a dominant entry point due to regulatory or cultural norms. In others, ESG has become the primary lens through which responsibility is evaluated, driven by investor pressure. Shared Value tends to emerge where innovation ecosystems and market maturity allow for deeper integration of social impact and business strategy. Effective organizations adapt their approach while maintaining a consistent ethical foundation.

For marketers, understanding ESG, CSR, and Shared Value is not merely theoretical. These frameworks shape brand trust, influence purchasing decisions, and determine how sustainability claims are interpreted. Marketing teams must work closely with leadership, operations, and compliance functions to ensure alignment between communication and reality. When frameworks are misunderstood or misrepresented, brands risk accusations of greenwashing or ethical inconsistency.

Importantly, none of these frameworks should be viewed as static or mutually exclusive. CSR initiatives can evolve into Shared Value strategies. ESG reporting can highlight areas where Shared Value innovation is needed. Together, they form a continuum of responsibility that reflects increasing sophistication and integration. Organizations that recognize this continuum are better positioned to adapt to evolving stakeholder expectations.

In a conscious consumer and investor landscape, responsibility is no longer a peripheral concern. ESG, CSR, and Shared Value each represent tools for navigating this reality, offering different lenses through which impact and performance can be understood. The challenge for modern organizations is not choosing one framework over another, but integrating them in a way that is authentic, measurable, and strategically aligned.

Ultimately, these frameworks reflect a broader shift in how success is defined. Profit remains essential, but it is no longer sufficient on its own. Businesses are judged by how they generate value, how they manage risk, and how they contribute to societal progress. ESG,

CSR, and Shared Value together provide a roadmap for meeting these expectations and building relevance in a world where responsibility and performance are increasingly inseparable.

## Sustainable Marketing vs. Green Marketing

The distinction between sustainable marketing and green marketing is subtle in language but substantial in practice, intent, and long-term impact. While the two terms are often used interchangeably in public discourse, they represent fundamentally different approaches to how brands engage with environmental and social responsibility. Understanding this distinction is critical in a conscious consumer world where credibility, accountability, and authenticity determine whether marketing efforts build trust or invite skepticism.

Green marketing emerged earlier as a response to rising environmental awareness. At its core, green marketing focuses on promoting products or services based on their environmental attributes. This may include claims related to eco-friendliness, energy efficiency, recyclability, reduced emissions, or use of natural ingredients. Green marketing is typically product-centric and communication-driven, highlighting specific features that reduce environmental harm compared to conventional alternatives. Its primary objective is to appeal to environmentally conscious consumers by positioning offerings as "better for the planet."

In its early form, green marketing played an important role in raising awareness about environmental issues and encouraging consumers to consider ecological impact in their purchasing decisions. It helped introduce concepts such as recycled packaging, organic materials, and energy-saving technologies into mainstream markets. For many companies, green marketing represented a first step toward acknowledging environmental responsibility and responding to emerging consumer concerns.

However, green marketing has historically been limited in scope. It often operates at the surface level of product attributes rather than addressing the broader systems in which products are designed, produced, and consumed. In many cases, green marketing focuses on isolated improvements without questioning underlying business models, consumption patterns, or long-term environmental impact. This narrow focus has made green marketing vulnerable to exaggeration, selective disclosure, and inconsistency.

One of the most significant challenges associated with green marketing is the risk of greenwashing. Greenwashing occurs when brands overstate or misrepresent their environmental efforts, using vague language, misleading imagery, or unsupported claims to create a perception of sustainability without substantive action. As consumer awareness has increased, greenwashing has become a major source of distrust, leading to regulatory scrutiny and reputational damage for companies that rely on superficial environmental messaging.

Sustainable marketing, by contrast, represents a more comprehensive and strategic approach. Rather than focusing solely on environmental claims, sustainable marketing integrates environmental, social, and economic considerations into the entire marketing ecosystem. It is not limited to how a product is promoted, but encompasses how it is designed, priced, distributed, communicated, and supported over time. Sustainable marketing aligns marketing objectives with long-term societal well-being and organizational responsibility.

At its core, sustainable marketing is grounded in systems thinking. It recognizes that marketing does not operate in isolation, but influences consumption patterns, resource use, cultural norms, and societal expectations. Sustainable marketing therefore seeks to balance customer needs, business goals, and broader impact. This approach moves beyond promoting "greener" products to questioning how value is created and delivered in a way that can be sustained over generations.

Another key distinction lies in intent. Green marketing is often tactical and reactive, responding to market trends or competitive pressure. Sustainable marketing is strategic and proactive, driven by a long-term vision of responsible growth. While green marketing asks how to sell an environmentally friendly product, sustainable marketing asks whether the product should exist in its current form, how it can be improved systemically, and how consumption itself can be guided more responsibly.

Sustainable marketing also differs in its relationship with transparency and accountability. Green marketing campaigns frequently rely on selective storytelling, highlighting positive aspects while omitting trade-offs or limitations. Sustainable marketing, in contrast, emphasizes honest communication, acknowledging complexities and challenges. It accepts that sustainability is a journey rather than a fixed state and communicates progress, setbacks, and commitments with clarity and evidence.

From an organizational perspective, green marketing is often confined to marketing or communications teams. Sustainable marketing requires cross-functional integration. Product development, supply chain management, operations, finance, and leadership must align with sustainability goals for marketing claims to be credible. This integration reduces the risk of inconsistency between what a brand says and what it does, which is a primary source of consumer distrust.

Consumer perception further highlights the difference between the two approaches. As consumers become more sophisticated, they increasingly differentiate between symbolic environmental claims and substantive commitment. Green marketing may attract attention in the short term, but it is less effective at building long-term trust if not supported by genuine practices. Sustainable marketing, when executed authentically, strengthens brand relationships by demonstrating consistency, responsibility, and shared values.

The scope of impact also varies significantly. Green marketing typically addresses environmental impact at the product level. Sustainable marketing addresses impact at the system level, including supply chains, labor practices, community engagement, and lifecycle outcomes. This broader scope reflects an understanding that environmental issues are interconnected with social and economic systems, and that meaningful change requires holistic solutions.

In terms of measurement, green marketing often relies on qualitative claims or limited certifications. Sustainable marketing is increasingly data-driven, aligned with ESG metrics, lifecycle assessments, and impact reporting. This emphasis on measurement supports accountability and enables stakeholders to evaluate performance objectively. It also helps organizations identify areas for improvement rather than relying on static claims.

Regulatory and legal considerations further differentiate the two. Green marketing has come under increasing scrutiny as governments and regulators seek to prevent misleading environmental claims. This has led to stricter guidelines around terminology, substantiation, and disclosure. Sustainable marketing, by embedding responsibility into operations rather than relying solely on claims, is better positioned to withstand regulatory pressure and adapt to evolving standards.

Another important distinction lies in how each approach views the consumer's role. Green marketing often treats consumers as end-users who can "do good" by choosing the right products. Sustainable marketing views consumers as partners in a broader transition toward responsible consumption. This perspective encourages education, engagement, and behavior change rather than simple transactional choices. It acknowledges that sustainability requires collaboration between brands and consumers rather than one-sided persuasion.

Sustainable marketing also addresses the issue of consumption volume, which green marketing often avoids. Promoting environmentally friendly products without addressing overconsumption can limit overall impact. Sustainable marketing recognizes that reducing harm may involve encouraging durability, reuse, repair, or even reduced consumption. This represents a more challenging but ultimately more credible approach to responsibility.

From a brand positioning standpoint, green marketing often competes on environmental superiority, emphasizing how one product is greener than another. Sustainable marketing competes on values alignment, trust, and long-term relevance. It seeks to build a brand identity rooted in responsibility rather than isolated environmental benefits. This positioning is more resilient to imitation and less dependent on specific claims that may become outdated over time.

The evolution from green marketing to sustainable marketing mirrors broader shifts in consumer expectations. Early environmental messaging focused on awareness and differentiation. Today's consumers expect integration, accountability, and impact. What was once considered progressive is now viewed as basic. As a result, green marketing alone is increasingly insufficient to meet stakeholder expectations.

This does not mean that green marketing has no role. Environmental product attributes remain important and relevant. However, in a sustainable marketing framework, these attributes are contextualized within a broader narrative of responsibility. Green marketing tactics can be effective when they are part of a genuine, organization-wide sustainability strategy rather than standalone efforts.

The consequences of confusing or conflating these approaches can be significant. Brands that rely on green marketing language without sustainable foundations risk reputational damage, consumer backlash, and loss of trust. Conversely, brands that invest in sustainable marketing but fail to communicate clearly may miss opportunities to engage and educate consumers. The challenge lies in aligning action and communication without overstating or oversimplifying impact.

For marketers, the shift from green marketing to sustainable marketing requires a change in mindset. It involves moving from persuasion to stewardship, from short-term campaigns to long-term commitment. Marketing becomes a tool not only for driving demand, but for shaping responsible consumption patterns and reinforcing organizational values.

Ultimately, the difference between sustainable marketing and green marketing reflects a deeper question about the role of business in society. Green marketing asks how to sell greener products within existing systems. Sustainable marketing asks how marketing itself can contribute to building systems that are environmentally sound, socially just, and economically viable. This broader ambition aligns more closely with the expectations of conscious consumers and the realities of global challenges.

In a world facing climate urgency, social inequality, and resource constraints, marketing cannot remain narrowly focused on promotion alone. Sustainable marketing offers a framework for aligning growth with responsibility, ensuring that marketing activity contributes positively rather than exacerbating existing problems. It represents an evolution in both practice and purpose.

As consumer scrutiny continues to intensify, the gap between green marketing and sustainable marketing will become increasingly visible. Brands that understand and embrace this distinction will be better equipped to build credibility, adapt to change, and maintain relevance. Those that do not risk being perceived as superficial or disconnected from the values shaping modern markets.

## Long-Term Brand Equity Through Sustainability

Long-term brand equity is built on trust, relevance, and consistent value creation over time. In the 21st century, sustainability has emerged as one of the most powerful drivers shaping all three of these dimensions. As consumers, investors, employees, and regulators increasingly evaluate brands through ethical and environmental lenses, sustainability is no longer a peripheral initiative but a central determinant of brand strength. Brands that embed sustainability into their core strategy are not merely responding to trends; they are investing in durable equity that compounds over years and decades.

Brand equity represents the intangible value a brand holds beyond its functional offerings. It is reflected in customer loyalty, price premium, advocacy, resilience during crises, and the ability to extend into new categories. Traditionally, brand equity was driven by awareness, perceived quality, associations, and emotional connection. While these elements remain relevant, sustainability now influences each of them in profound ways. A brand's stance on environmental stewardship, social responsibility, and ethical conduct increasingly shapes how it is perceived and remembered.

Sustainability contributes to long-term brand equity by reinforcing trust. Trust is the foundation of any enduring brand relationship, and it is built through consistency between words and actions. When brands demonstrate genuine commitment to sustainable practices—such as responsible sourcing, fair labor standards, emissions reduction, or community investment—they signal reliability and integrity. Over time, this consistency strengthens consumer confidence, making the brand a dependable choice in an uncertain world.

In contrast to short-term promotional tactics, sustainability-driven brand building operates on a longer horizon. It requires patience, investment, and a willingness to prioritize long-term value over immediate gains. Brands that take this approach are often rewarded with deeper loyalty, as consumers increasingly favor companies that align with their values. This loyalty is more resilient than transactional preference because it is rooted in shared beliefs rather than price or convenience alone.

One of the most significant ways sustainability enhances brand equity is by strengthening emotional connection. Modern consumers do not simply buy products; they buy into narratives, identities, and causes. Brands that articulate a clear sustainability purpose provide consumers with a sense of participation in something meaningful. This emotional resonance transforms consumption into expression, allowing customers to signal their values through brand choice.

This emotional dimension is particularly important in competitive markets where functional differentiation is limited. When products are similar in quality and price, sustainability becomes a powerful differentiator. A brand perceived as responsible, ethical, and forward-thinking stands out not because of what it sells, but because of what it represents. Over time, these associations accumulate, enhancing brand recall and preference.

Sustainability also supports long-term brand equity by future-proofing relevance. Consumer expectations are not static; they evolve alongside social, environmental, and economic realities. Brands that anticipate these shifts and adapt proactively are better positioned to remain relevant. Sustainability-driven brands are often more agile because they monitor emerging risks, regulatory changes, and societal concerns as part of their strategic planning.

This forward-looking orientation reduces vulnerability to disruption. For example, brands that invest early in sustainable materials or low-carbon processes are less exposed to supply chain shocks, resource scarcity, or regulatory penalties. While these operational benefits are tangible, their impact on brand equity is equally important. Stakeholders perceive such brands as responsible and prepared, reinforcing confidence in their long-term viability.

From a reputation management perspective, sustainability acts as a buffer during crises. No brand is immune to mistakes or external challenges, but those with a strong sustainability track record often receive greater benefit of the doubt. Stakeholders are more willing to forgive missteps when they believe a brand's intentions are sincere and its values are consistent. This reputational resilience is a critical component of long-term brand equity.

Sustainability-driven brand equity also extends beyond consumers to other key stakeholders. Employees increasingly seek purpose-driven organizations, and employer brand plays a significant role in attracting and retaining talent. Companies known for ethical practices, inclusivity, and environmental responsibility are more likely to engage motivated employees who become brand ambassadors. This internal alignment strengthens external perception, creating a virtuous cycle of credibility and advocacy.

Investors, too, increasingly factor sustainability into their assessment of brand value. Environmental, social, and governance performance is now closely linked to perceptions of risk, stability, and long-term growth potential. Brands with strong sustainability credentials are often viewed as better managed and more resilient, which enhances overall brand valuation. This financial dimension reinforces the strategic importance of sustainability in brand equity creation.

Long-term brand equity through sustainability also depends on authenticity. Superficial or inconsistent efforts can undermine trust and erode brand value. Conscious consumers are adept at identifying greenwashing and symbolic gestures that lack substance. Sustainable brand equity is therefore built not through grand claims, but through credible actions supported by transparent communication and measurable outcomes.

Transparency plays a central role in this process. Brands that openly share progress, challenges, and trade-offs demonstrate honesty and accountability. Rather than weakening brand equity, this openness often strengthens it by signaling maturity and responsibility. Consumers increasingly appreciate brands that acknowledge imperfections and show commitment to continuous improvement rather than presenting an unrealistic image of perfection.

Another important dimension of sustainability-driven brand equity is longevity. Sustainable brands tend to emphasize durability, quality, and long-term use over planned obsolescence. This focus not only reduces environmental impact but also reinforces perceptions of reliability and value. Products that last longer and perform consistently contribute to positive brand experiences that accumulate over time.

The ability to command price premiums is another indicator of strong brand equity influenced by sustainability. Consumers are often willing to pay more for brands they trust and respect, particularly when sustainability benefits are clear and credible. While price sensitivity varies across markets, sustainability-driven premiums are most effective when they are justified through quality, transparency, and demonstrated impact rather than moral pressure alone.

Sustainability also enhances brand equity by enabling meaningful storytelling. Brands with genuine sustainability initiatives have richer narratives to share—stories of innovation, collaboration, and positive change. These stories humanize brands and create emotional touchpoints that go beyond product features. Over time, consistent storytelling reinforces brand identity and strengthens memory structures in the consumer's mind.

However, it is important to recognize that sustainability is not a quick fix for brand equity challenges. It cannot compensate for poor product quality, unethical behavior, or inconsistent customer experience. Instead, sustainability amplifies existing strengths or weaknesses. When aligned with strong fundamentals, it accelerates brand equity growth; when misaligned, it exposes gaps between promise and reality.

The integration of sustainability into brand strategy requires alignment across touchpoints. Advertising, packaging, customer service, digital presence, and corporate behavior must reflect the same values. Fragmentation undermines credibility and dilutes brand equity. Long-term success depends on coherence—ensuring that sustainability is not a campaign theme but a guiding principle across the brand ecosystem.

Cultural and regional contexts also influence how sustainability contributes to brand equity. While the underlying values of responsibility and ethics are broadly shared, their expression varies across markets. Brands that adapt their sustainability narratives to local priorities without compromising core principles are better positioned to build equity globally. This balance between consistency and relevance is essential for multinational brands.

Measurement is another critical factor in linking sustainability to long-term brand equity. Traditional brand metrics such as awareness and preference must be complemented by indicators of trust, credibility, and perceived impact. Longitudinal tracking helps organizations understand how sustainability initiatives influence brand perception over time rather than relying on short-term campaign results.

As sustainability becomes more mainstream, its role in brand equity will continue to evolve. What differentiates brands today may become a baseline expectation tomorrow. This raises the bar for continuous innovation and deeper impact. Long-term brand equity will increasingly depend on leadership—brands that set standards, influence behavior, and contribute meaningfully to systemic change.

Ultimately, sustainability strengthens brand equity by aligning business success with societal progress. It creates brands that are not only admired, but respected; not only chosen, but trusted. This alignment fosters relationships that endure beyond market fluctuations and shifting trends.

In a conscious consumer world, brand equity is no longer built solely on visibility or persuasion. It is built on credibility, contribution, and consistency over time. Sustainability provides the framework through which brands can earn and sustain this equity, transforming marketing from a tool of influence into a force for long-term value creation.

## Measuring Impact Beyond Profit

For much of modern business history, profit has been the primary measure of success. Financial performance determined whether strategies were effective, brands were strong, and organizations were sustainable in a narrow economic sense. However, as global challenges such as climate change, social inequality, and resource scarcity have intensified, this singular focus on profit has proven insufficient. Measuring impact beyond profit has become essential for understanding true organizational performance and long-term value creation.

Measuring impact beyond profit means evaluating how a business affects society, the environment, and broader economic systems, in addition to its financial outcomes. It recognizes that companies operate within complex ecosystems and that their actions create consequences—both positive and negative—that extend far beyond balance sheets. This broader perspective reflects a growing consensus that financial success and societal well-being are deeply interconnected rather than opposing goals.

One of the key reasons profit alone is no longer adequate is that it fails to capture externalities. Externalities are costs or benefits imposed on society that are not reflected in a company's financial statements. Environmental pollution, carbon emissions, labor exploitation, and community displacement may not immediately affect profitability, yet they generate long-term risks and societal harm. Measuring impact beyond profit seeks to make these hidden effects visible and manageable.

The shift toward broader impact measurement has been driven in part by changing stakeholder expectations. Consumers, employees, investors, regulators, and communities increasingly demand transparency about how companies generate profits. They want to know not just whether a company is successful, but whether its success is responsible, ethical, and sustainable. This shift has expanded the definition of value from purely financial returns to shared value across stakeholders.

Environmental impact measurement is one of the most established components of impact beyond profit. Metrics such as carbon footprint, water usage, waste generation, and energy efficiency help organizations understand their ecological impact. These measures provide insight into resource dependency, operational efficiency, and exposure to environmental risks. Over time, they also guide innovation toward more sustainable processes and products.

Social impact measurement focuses on how businesses affect people—employees, customers, suppliers, and communities. This includes labor practices, workplace diversity and inclusion, health and safety, human rights, and community engagement. Measuring social impact helps organizations identify whether their operations contribute to equitable opportunity or reinforce systemic inequalities. It also highlights risks related to talent retention, reputation, and social license to operate.

Economic impact beyond profit examines how value is distributed rather than simply generated. This includes fair wages, supplier relationships, local economic development, and tax practices. While profit measures what a company earns, economic impact metrics assess how that wealth contributes to broader economic stability and resilience. This perspective is particularly relevant in discussions around inclusive growth and responsible capitalism.

Frameworks such as the triple bottom line have played an important role in formalizing this expanded view of performance. The triple bottom line evaluates success across three dimensions: people, planet, and profit. While not without limitations, it helped shift business thinking toward integrated measurement and highlighted the interdependence of financial, social, and environmental outcomes.

More recently, standardized reporting frameworks have emerged to support consistent and credible impact measurement. ESG metrics, sustainability reporting standards, and integrated reporting models aim to provide comparable data on non-financial performance. These frameworks help organizations move beyond anecdotal claims toward evidence-based evaluation, enabling stakeholders to assess progress and hold companies accountable.

However, measuring impact beyond profit presents significant challenges. Unlike financial metrics, many social and environmental outcomes are complex, long-term, and difficult to quantify. For example, assessing the impact of diversity initiatives or community programs requires qualitative analysis alongside quantitative data. This complexity demands new skills, interdisciplinary approaches, and a willingness to embrace uncertainty.

Another challenge lies in attribution. Businesses often struggle to determine how much of a particular outcome can be directly attributed to their actions versus broader systemic factors. Measuring impact beyond profit therefore requires careful methodology and transparency about assumptions. The goal is not perfect precision, but credible insight that informs better decision-making.

Despite these challenges, impact measurement offers strategic advantages. By tracking non-financial performance, organizations gain early warning signals about emerging risks. Environmental data can reveal exposure to regulatory changes or resource scarcity. Social metrics can highlight cultural issues that may affect productivity or brand reputation. In this way, impact measurement strengthens risk management and strategic resilience.

Measuring impact beyond profit also supports innovation. When companies understand the environmental and social costs of their operations, they are more likely to explore alternative materials, processes, and business models. Impact data provides direction for innovation efforts, aligning creativity with responsibility rather than short-term optimization alone.

From a marketing perspective, impact measurement enhances credibility. Conscious consumers are increasingly skeptical of vague claims and aspirational language. Demonstrating measurable outcomes—such as emissions reductions, fair sourcing percentages, or community investment results—builds trust and differentiates authentic commitment from superficial messaging. Impact data becomes a foundation for transparent storytelling rather than promotional exaggeration.

Internal alignment is another important benefit. When organizations measure impact beyond profit, they create shared goals that unite departments around a broader purpose. Employees are more engaged when they can see how their work contributes to positive outcomes. Clear metrics help translate abstract values into concrete actions and accountability across teams.

Investors have also played a significant role in accelerating impact measurement. Long-term investors increasingly recognize that environmental and social performance influence financial stability and growth. By evaluating impact metrics alongside financial results, investors gain a more comprehensive understanding of risk and opportunity. This integration reinforces the idea that measuring impact beyond profit is not anti-business, but pro-sustainability.

It is important to distinguish meaningful impact measurement from box-ticking exercises. Simply collecting data without integrating insights into strategy limits value. Measuring impact beyond profit is most effective when it informs decisions, influences incentives, and shapes organizational priorities. The goal is not reporting for its own sake, but continuous improvement guided by evidence.

Transparency is central to this process. Sharing impact data openly—along with limitations and areas for improvement—signals accountability and maturity. While transparency may expose shortcomings, it also builds credibility and invites collaboration. Stakeholders are more likely to trust organizations that acknowledge challenges than those that present an unrealistic image of perfection.

Over time, impact measurement can redefine success itself. When leaders evaluate performance through a broader lens, strategic trade-offs change. Decisions that may reduce short-term profit but create long-term societal value become more acceptable. This shift supports sustainable growth rather than extractive models that undermine future viability.

Cultural context also shapes how impact is measured and valued. Different regions prioritize different social and environmental issues based on local realities. Effective impact measurement balances global standards with local relevance, ensuring that metrics reflect meaningful outcomes rather than abstract benchmarks detached from lived experience.

Technology is increasingly enabling more sophisticated impact measurement. Data analytics, digital monitoring, and lifecycle assessment tools allow organizations to track complex systems with greater accuracy. While technology does not eliminate judgment, it enhances the ability to identify patterns, evaluate trade-offs, and measure progress over time.

As expectations continue to evolve, measuring impact beyond profit will become less of a differentiator and more of a baseline requirement. Organizations that fail to adopt broader measurement frameworks risk being perceived as outdated or irresponsible.

Conversely, those that lead in impact measurement help shape norms, standards, and best practices across industries.

Ultimately, measuring impact beyond profit reflects a fundamental shift in how success is defined. It acknowledges that businesses are not isolated entities, but participants in shared social and environmental systems. Profit remains essential, but it is no longer sufficient as the sole indicator of performance.

# The Business Case for Sustainable Marketing

## Financial Performance and Sustainable Brands

Financial performance and sustainable brands are deeply interconnected, though the relationship is often misunderstood. Historically, sustainability was viewed as an added cost—a trade-off between ethical responsibility and profitability. Companies were expected to choose between doing good and doing well. In recent decades, however, evidence has increasingly demonstrated that sustainable practices are not merely compatible with financial performance—they can actively enhance it. For sustainable brands, environmental stewardship, social responsibility, and ethical governance are drivers of long-term value creation rather than liabilities.

Financial performance in the context of sustainable brands encompasses traditional metrics such as revenue growth, profitability, and return on investment, while also integrating long-term resilience and risk mitigation. Sustainable brands tend to perform better financially over time because they proactively address risks that can erode profit, such as regulatory penalties, resource scarcity, supply chain disruptions, and reputational damage. By embedding sustainability into strategy, brands reduce exposure to these threats and position themselves for stable, enduring performance.

Consumer behavior is one of the most significant drivers linking sustainability to financial outcomes. Conscious consumers increasingly prefer brands that demonstrate ethical, social, and environmental responsibility. They are willing to pay a premium for products that align with their values, which directly boosts revenue and margins. Furthermore, these consumers are more likely to remain loyal, act as brand advocates, and tolerate occasional service or price fluctuations, all of which contribute to long-term financial stability. Sustainable branding, therefore, creates both demand-side advantages and enhanced customer lifetime value.

Operational efficiency is another channel through which sustainable brands improve financial performance. Sustainability initiatives often lead to cost savings by optimizing resource use, reducing waste, improving energy efficiency, and streamlining logistics. For instance, transitioning to renewable energy or implementing circular supply chains may require upfront investment but can significantly reduce operating costs over time. These operational improvements directly impact profitability while simultaneously enhancing environmental performance.

Risk management and regulatory compliance are critical factors as well. Governments, investors, and international agencies increasingly impose standards for environmental and social responsibility. Brands that integrate sustainability into their core operations are better prepared to comply with evolving regulations, avoid fines, and capitalize on incentives such as tax benefits or green financing. Such proactive measures protect revenue streams and reduce the likelihood of unexpected financial liabilities.

Investor perception also plays a growing role in connecting sustainability to financial performance. Environmental, Social, and Governance (ESG) metrics are increasingly incorporated into investment decisions, with many studies showing that companies with strong ESG performance experience lower cost of capital, higher market valuation, and more favorable financing conditions. Sustainable brands are perceived as lower-risk, forward-thinking, and better managed, which strengthens investor confidence and access to capital.

Brand reputation and trust, which are integral to sustainable branding, have tangible financial implications. A positive reputation can drive sales, facilitate partnerships, and enable market expansion. Conversely, brands associated with environmental harm, social injustice, or unethical practices are increasingly vulnerable to boycotts, activism, and negative media coverage, all of which can erode revenue and market share. Sustainable brands proactively cultivate goodwill, translating ethical credibility into measurable financial benefits.

Innovation is another pathway linking sustainability to financial performance. Sustainable brands frequently explore product, service, and business model innovations that meet emerging consumer demands and regulatory expectations. For example, companies developing low-carbon products, socially inclusive services, or circular economy solutions can capture new market segments, differentiate from competitors, and create additional revenue streams. Innovation driven by sustainability thus becomes both a growth engine and a mechanism for maintaining long-term financial health.

Employee engagement and retention further contribute to financial performance. Sustainable brands are often perceived as more attractive employers, particularly among younger, purpose-driven talent. High levels of engagement improve productivity, reduce turnover, and lower recruitment costs. In addition, employees aligned with the company's sustainability values are more likely to act as brand ambassadors, enhancing marketing effectiveness and reinforcing the brand's ethical image in the marketplace.

Supply chain resilience is another financial advantage of sustainability. Brands that prioritize ethical sourcing, supplier environmental standards, and risk diversification are less exposed to disruptions, reputational crises, or volatile pricing. A sustainable supply chain supports consistent production, cost stability, and reliable delivery—factors that directly impact revenue and operational profitability.

Moreover, financial performance benefits from long-term strategic alignment between sustainability and brand positioning. Sustainable brands are better able to anticipate societal trends, policy shifts, and consumer expectations, reducing the risk of obsolescence. This foresight supports strategic investments that maximize return over time, rather than short-term profits that may undermine ethical or environmental goals. In this sense, sustainability acts as both a protective measure and a value multiplier for brand equity.

Empirical studies increasingly support the link between sustainability and financial outcomes. Research has shown that brands with robust sustainability strategies often outperform peers on stock performance, profitability, and market share. This correlation demonstrates that ethical responsibility, when integrated authentically into business practices, can coexist with—and even enhance—economic success.

It is important to note that financial gains from sustainability are rarely immediate. The benefits accrue over time through brand loyalty, operational efficiency, innovation, risk reduction, and market differentiation. Companies that view sustainability as a short-term marketing tactic rather than a strategic commitment may fail to realize its full financial potential. True sustainable brands embed responsibility into every facet of operations, ensuring that financial performance is reinforced rather than compromised.

Finally, sustainability-driven financial performance enhances resilience in a rapidly changing global landscape. As consumer expectations, regulatory environments, and environmental realities evolve, brands anchored in sustainability are better positioned to adapt, maintain relevance, and protect shareholder value. This adaptability is a critical component of long-term financial health, particularly in markets characterized by volatility, disruption, and increasing societal scrutiny.

## Risk Mitigation and Regulatory Alignment

Risk mitigation and regulatory alignment are critical components of sustainable business strategy, particularly in a world where consumer expectations, governmental regulations, and investor scrutiny are intensifying. Companies can no longer view sustainability as a peripheral initiative; it is increasingly central to operational resilience, legal compliance, and strategic decision-making. Integrating sustainability into risk management and regulatory alignment allows organizations to anticipate potential threats, safeguard reputation, and maintain long-term financial and operational stability.

Risk mitigation in the context of sustainability involves identifying, assessing, and managing the environmental, social, and governance (ESG) risks that could impact an organization's operations, reputation, or financial performance. Environmental risks may include resource scarcity, climate-related events, pollution liabilities, or regulatory penalties for non-compliance with emissions standards. Social risks encompass labor disputes, human rights violations, community opposition, and negative stakeholder perception. Governance risks involve inadequate oversight, ethical lapses, corruption, or failure to adhere to internal and external policies. By proactively managing these risks, sustainable organizations reduce the likelihood of costly disruptions and enhance resilience against unforeseen challenges.

A sustainable risk mitigation strategy begins with a comprehensive assessment of vulnerabilities across the supply chain, operations, and broader market context. For example, companies dependent on raw materials from regions vulnerable to climate change may experience supply disruptions or price volatility. By identifying these risks early, organizations can implement strategies such as diversified sourcing, investment in alternative materials, or supply chain collaboration to maintain continuity. This proactive approach reduces operational and financial exposure while demonstrating foresight to stakeholders.

Regulatory alignment complements risk mitigation by ensuring that organizations operate within legal frameworks and anticipate future compliance requirements. Environmental and social regulations are becoming more stringent globally, with governments implementing laws on emissions, waste management, labor standards, product labeling, and corporate transparency. Aligning operations with these requirements not only prevents legal penalties but also positions companies as responsible market participants. For instance, adherence to international standards like ISO 14001 (environmental management) or SA8000 (social accountability) can enhance credibility, reduce audit risks, and facilitate access to global markets.

The relationship between risk mitigation and regulatory alignment is mutually reinforcing. Compliance with regulations reduces exposure to legal and financial penalties, while comprehensive risk management identifies areas where regulations may evolve, allowing companies to stay ahead of requirements. For example, understanding the risk of future carbon taxes enables organizations to invest in low-emission technologies proactively rather than reacting after the imposition of a regulatory burden. This anticipatory approach demonstrates leadership and reduces the cost of compliance over time.

Investor expectations increasingly tie risk management and regulatory alignment to financial performance. ESG-focused investors scrutinize how well companies anticipate regulatory changes, manage environmental and social risks, and integrate these considerations into strategy. Firms with robust risk mitigation and compliance practices often enjoy lower capital costs, higher valuations, and stronger access to financing. Conversely, companies that fail to align with evolving regulations may face divestment, reputational damage, or higher insurance and borrowing costs.

Transparency and reporting are central to both risk mitigation and regulatory alignment. Companies are expected to provide clear, accurate, and verifiable disclosures about their sustainability risks and compliance efforts. Frameworks such as the Global Reporting Initiative (GRI), Sustainability Accounting Standards Board (SASB), and Task Force on Climate-related Financial Disclosures (TCFD) provide structured approaches for communicating risk management and regulatory alignment. Transparent reporting reassures stakeholders that sustainability is integrated into strategy rather than being superficial or reactive.

Reputation management is another important aspect. Organizations that effectively mitigate risks and comply with regulations are perceived as responsible, trustworthy, and resilient. This perception strengthens brand equity, attracts conscious consumers, and builds loyalty. Conversely, failure to manage sustainability risks or comply with regulations can result in public backlash, litigation, or boycotts, which can erode both revenue and long-term brand value.

Sustainable risk mitigation also extends to innovation and operational planning. Anticipating regulatory changes or ESG-related risks encourages companies to innovate in products, processes, and business models. For example, stricter environmental regulations may incentivize investment in renewable energy, sustainable packaging, or circular supply chains. These innovations reduce exposure to regulatory penalties, improve efficiency, and open new market opportunities, simultaneously mitigating risk and enhancing competitive advantage.

Cross-functional integration is essential for effective risk mitigation and regulatory alignment. Sustainability considerations must be embedded across departments—legal, operations, procurement, finance, marketing, and R&D—to ensure comprehensive identification and management of risks. Isolated initiatives may address certain risks but fail to capture systemic vulnerabilities, whereas integrated approaches enable proactive management and coordinated response.

Cultural and regional variations in regulations and stakeholder expectations further emphasize the need for alignment. Multinational organizations must navigate diverse legal frameworks and social norms, adapting their sustainability strategies accordingly. Companies that maintain flexibility while upholding core ethical standards are better equipped to manage risk across global operations.

Scenario planning and stress testing are additional tools for sustainable risk management. By modeling potential environmental, social, and regulatory shocks, companies can prepare contingency plans and allocate resources efficiently. For instance, simulating the financial impact of carbon pricing, supply chain disruptions, or labor unrest allows decision-makers to implement mitigation strategies before crises occur. This proactive planning strengthens resilience and reduces uncertainty in financial forecasting.

Ultimately, risk mitigation and regulatory alignment are not just defensive measures—they are strategic enablers. Organizations that integrate sustainability into risk management gain a competitive advantage by avoiding disruptions, maintaining stakeholder trust, reducing costs, and identifying growth opportunities. They are better positioned to capitalize on emerging regulations, evolving consumer preferences, and investor expectations.

# Investor Expectations and Market Valuation

Investor expectations and market valuation are increasingly influenced by sustainability considerations, reflecting a fundamental shift in how capital markets assess corporate value. Traditional investment analysis primarily focused on financial metrics such as revenue growth, profitability, and cash flow. While these remain important, investors now recognize that long-term performance is closely tied to a company's environmental, social, and governance (ESG) practices, ethical conduct, and resilience to societal and environmental changes. For sustainable brands, meeting investor expectations is not just about compliance—it is a strategic imperative that directly affects market valuation and access to capital.

Investor expectations in the context of sustainability are multifaceted. Investors seek transparency, accountability, and credible reporting on ESG performance. They expect companies to identify and manage material risks, such as climate change, labor practices, regulatory exposure, and supply chain vulnerabilities. Additionally, investors are looking for opportunities where sustainability drives innovation, competitive advantage, and long-term growth. Brands that integrate sustainability into strategy are perceived as forward-looking, reducing risk and increasing the likelihood of stable, long-term returns.

Sustainability-driven investor expectations also extend to corporate governance and ethical behavior. Investors evaluate leadership integrity, board oversight, and alignment between executive incentives and long-term value creation. Companies that demonstrate ethical governance practices are seen as less prone to scandal, regulatory penalties, or operational disruption. In contrast, organizations with weak governance or inconsistent sustainability performance may be viewed as risky, which can lead to lower market confidence and diminished valuation.

Market valuation is directly affected by how well companies meet these evolving expectations. Studies have shown that firms with robust ESG practices often enjoy higher stock prices, lower cost of capital, and greater investor confidence. Positive perception of sustainability performance signals long-term stability, innovation potential, and reduced exposure to environmental or social risks. Consequently, these companies are often valued more favorably than peers with similar financial metrics but weaker sustainability credentials.

The relationship between investor expectations and market valuation is reinforced through mechanisms such as ESG ratings, sustainability indices, and reporting frameworks. Investors increasingly rely on standardized ESG metrics to assess risk, performance, and future potential. Ratings from agencies like MSCI, Sustainalytics, or FTSE Russell provide benchmarks that influence investment decisions, portfolio allocation, and shareholder engagement. Companies that perform well on these metrics often experience enhanced market visibility, improved liquidity, and stronger investor demand.

Long-term financial performance is also influenced by sustainability-aligned investment. Investors who prioritize ESG are generally more patient and willing to support companies with strategic, long-term initiatives, even if short-term profits are moderated by sustainability investments. This enables sustainable brands to pursue innovation, operational efficiency, and social impact without being pressured to prioritize immediate gains over future growth. Such alignment between capital and purpose enhances resilience and can contribute to superior long-term returns.

Risk mitigation, which intersects with investor expectations, plays a critical role in market valuation. Companies that actively manage environmental, social, and governance risks reduce the likelihood of unexpected liabilities, regulatory penalties, or reputational crises. This proactive approach reassures investors, reduces perceived risk, and supports higher valuation multiples. Conversely, companies that fail to address ESG risks may face higher volatility in stock price, reduced access to capital, and increased investor scrutiny.

Transparency and reporting are also central to meeting investor expectations and supporting valuation. Investors demand clear, credible disclosure of sustainability performance, including both achievements and challenges. Frameworks such as the Global Reporting Initiative (GRI), Sustainability Accounting Standards Board (SASB), and Task Force on Climate-related Financial Disclosures (TCFD) provide standardized approaches that enhance comparability and reduce information asymmetry. Brands that excel in transparent reporting are more likely to earn investor trust, which translates into improved market valuation.

Consumer behavior indirectly influences investor perception as well. Companies with strong sustainability credentials often attract loyal, conscious consumers, which can translate into revenue growth, brand resilience, and market differentiation. Investors recognize that consumer trust and loyalty strengthen financial performance and reduce the risk of market volatility, further reinforcing the link between sustainability and valuation.

Investor expectations are also increasingly global in scope. Multinational investors consider not only domestic regulations and norms but also international standards, supply chain practices, and cross-border ESG performance. Companies that align with global sustainability expectations are better positioned to access international capital markets, attract foreign investment, and maintain competitive positioning. Market valuation is therefore sensitive to both local and global sustainability performance.

Furthermore, the integration of sustainability into strategic planning can influence long-term market valuation through innovation and competitive advantage. Sustainable brands that develop eco-friendly products, socially responsible services, or circular business models often create new revenue streams and capture emerging markets. Investors perceive these initiatives as indicators of growth potential and strategic foresight, supporting higher valuation multiples.

It is important to note that investor expectations are not static; they evolve alongside regulatory changes, societal awareness, and technological advances. Companies must continuously monitor market trends, stakeholder sentiment, and policy developments to maintain alignment. Brands that adapt proactively are rewarded with higher investor confidence and valuation stability, while those that lag may face divestment, lower stock prices, or increased scrutiny.

The interplay between investor expectations and market valuation also underscores the importance of authenticity. Superficial sustainability claims or greenwashing can damage credibility, erode investor trust, and depress market value. In contrast, genuine, evidence-based initiatives strengthen confidence, enhance valuation, and position the company as a reliable, forward-looking investment.

Finally, sustainable brands that meet investor expectations and achieve favorable market valuation create a virtuous cycle. Higher valuation provides access to capital, which can be reinvested in further sustainability initiatives, innovation, and market expansion. Positive financial performance reinforces stakeholder confidence, creating momentum that strengthens both reputation and economic resilience.

## Customer Loyalty and Lifetime Value

Customer loyalty and lifetime value (CLV) are central metrics in evaluating the long-term success of any brand, and in the context of sustainability, they take on heightened strategic significance. Sustainable brands are uniquely positioned to cultivate deeper emotional connections with consumers, which directly strengthens loyalty and extends the financial and relational lifetime value of each customer. Understanding this relationship is crucial for marketers seeking to translate sustainability efforts into tangible business outcomes.

Customer loyalty refers to a consumer's consistent preference for a particular brand over time. It is characterized by repeat purchases, positive advocacy, and resistance to competitive offers. Loyalty is not merely a transactional phenomenon; it reflects trust, satisfaction, and alignment of values. In a conscious consumer world, sustainability plays a critical role in shaping loyalty because many consumers now evaluate brands based on ethical, social, and environmental behavior as much as product quality or price. Brands that demonstrate authentic commitment to sustainability signal shared values, which creates a deeper emotional bond with customers.

Sustainability-driven loyalty manifests in multiple ways. First, repeat purchases increase as consumers feel confident that the brand's practices align with their values. Second, loyal customers are more likely to act as brand advocates, sharing positive experiences within their social circles or on digital platforms, thereby generating organic marketing reach. Third, loyalty reduces price sensitivity; consumers committed to sustainability-aligned brands are often willing to pay a premium for ethically produced goods or services, which directly impacts profitability.

Customer lifetime value (CLV) measures the total revenue a brand can expect from a customer over the entirety of their relationship. CLV is influenced by purchase frequency, transaction value, and retention rate. When sustainability strengthens loyalty, it directly increases CLV by extending the duration and depth of engagement. For example, a customer who trusts a brand's ethical sourcing, environmental stewardship, or social responsibility is more likely to continue purchasing, upgrade to higher-value products, and explore complementary offerings. This cumulative value is far greater than that generated by one-time or transaction-focused purchases.

Sustainable practices enhance CLV not only through repeat purchase behavior but also by reducing churn risk. Brands perceived as irresponsible or misaligned with consumer values face higher attrition rates, whereas brands demonstrating authentic sustainability retain customers more effectively. Retention, in turn, reduces acquisition costs and increases profitability per customer, creating a favorable long-term financial trajectory.

Emotional engagement is a key mechanism linking sustainability to loyalty and CLV. Conscious consumers derive personal satisfaction from supporting brands that contribute positively to society and the environment. This sense of purpose reinforces habitual purchasing behavior and strengthens resistance to competing offers, even when competitors provide similar functional benefits. Over time, this emotional connection becomes a powerful driver of lifetime value.

Transparency and accountability amplify the effect of sustainability on loyalty and CLV. Brands that openly communicate their sustainability commitments, progress, and challenges foster trust. This transparency reassures customers that their purchases are contributing to genuine impact, further deepening loyalty. Conversely, inconsistent messaging or greenwashing can erode trust, reduce repeat purchases, and negatively affect CLV.

Another dimension is community engagement and co-creation. Brands that involve customers in sustainability initiatives—such as recycling programs, carbon-offset contributions, or social impact campaigns—create participatory experiences that strengthen relational bonds. These interactions transform consumers from passive purchasers into engaged advocates, increasing both loyalty and lifetime value through repeated engagement and social amplification.

Operational consistency also matters. Sustainable brands must deliver on their promises across the entire customer journey. Ethical sourcing, eco-friendly packaging, energy-efficient delivery, and responsible product lifecycle management must all align with communicated sustainability values. Any misalignment can damage loyalty and reduce lifetime value, while consistent execution reinforces trust and encourages sustained engagement.

Marketing and communication strategies amplify these effects. Storytelling that highlights tangible sustainability initiatives, measurable impact, and authentic leadership resonates with conscious consumers. When customers understand and appreciate how their purchases support meaningful outcomes, they are more likely to remain loyal and maximize their lifetime engagement with the brand.

Employee engagement indirectly contributes to customer loyalty and CLV. Employees aligned with sustainability values provide better service, communicate authentically, and embody the brand's ethical identity. Positive employee-customer interactions reinforce trust and satisfaction, which further strengthens loyalty and extends lifetime value.

Moreover, loyalty fueled by sustainability is often more resilient during economic fluctuations or competitive pressure. Customers who identify strongly with a brand's purpose are less likely to switch for minor price differences or convenience factors. This stability reduces volatility in revenue streams and enhances predictability in long-term financial planning.

Data-driven insights can further enhance the relationship between sustainability, loyalty, and CLV. Brands can track purchasing patterns, engagement with sustainability programs, and advocacy behavior to optimize strategies that increase retention and lifetime value. These analytics help identify which sustainability initiatives are most effective at fostering loyalty and inform resource allocation for maximum impact.

Globalization and cultural differences also influence loyalty and lifetime value. Consumers in different regions may prioritize environmental, social, or ethical dimensions differently. Sustainable brands that adapt initiatives and communications to resonate with local values while maintaining authenticity are more likely to generate loyalty and maximize CLV across diverse markets.

Finally, sustainability-driven loyalty and lifetime value are mutually reinforcing. High CLV provides resources for reinvestment in sustainability initiatives, further enhancing customer engagement and trust. Similarly, loyal and engaged customers contribute to organic advocacy and growth, creating a virtuous cycle where sustainability strengthens financial performance while building meaningful, long-term relationships.

# Competitive Advantage in Crowded Markets

Competitive advantage in crowded markets is increasingly defined not only by product quality, pricing, or convenience, but by a brand's ability to differentiate itself through sustainability. In highly saturated industries, where functional features are easily replicated, conscious consumers are seeking deeper connections with brands that align with their values. Sustainable practices—environmental stewardship, ethical sourcing, social responsibility—offer a compelling way to stand out, build trust, and create meaningful differentiation that competitors cannot easily imitate.

Traditional competitive advantage often relies on cost leadership, product innovation, or marketing reach. While these remain important, they are increasingly insufficient in markets where multiple players offer similar functional value. Sustainability provides an additional dimension that appeals to the growing segment of conscious consumers. Brands that embed responsible practices into product design, supply chains, and corporate culture can distinguish themselves by demonstrating authenticity, ethical behavior, and long-term commitment to societal impact.

One way sustainability drives competitive advantage is through brand reputation. Consumers are more likely to trust and recommend brands that show genuine concern for social and environmental issues. A strong reputation reduces perceived risk and strengthens loyalty, creating an edge over competitors who may offer similar products but lack credible ethical commitments. This reputational advantage translates directly into customer preference, higher willingness to pay, and increased market share.

Operational efficiency derived from sustainability also contributes to competitive advantage. Practices such as resource optimization, energy efficiency, and waste reduction not only lower costs but can also improve product quality and reliability. Brands that can deliver high-quality, responsibly produced goods at competitive prices gain both functional and ethical advantages in the marketplace. This dual value proposition is particularly effective in crowded markets, where differentiation is critical.

Sustainability-driven innovation is another source of advantage. Brands committed to ethical and environmental goals are often at the forefront of product, service, and business model innovation. This includes developing eco-friendly materials, circular supply chains, low-carbon logistics, or socially inclusive services. By continuously innovating around sustainability, brands can access new customer segments, create unique offerings, and establish barriers to entry that competitors find difficult to overcome.

Employee engagement and talent attraction also play a role in sustaining competitive advantage. Companies known for ethical and sustainable practices attract motivated, purpose-driven employees. Highly engaged employees are more productive, innovative, and committed to delivering exceptional customer experiences. This internal advantage enhances external brand perception, creating a reinforcing loop of operational excellence and customer trust.

Another key factor is regulatory foresight. Brands that proactively align with current and anticipated environmental and social regulations reduce compliance risk and avoid costly penalties. This not only protects profitability but also allows such brands to move faster than competitors in adapting to new standards, turning regulatory compliance into a strategic advantage rather than a burden.

Sustainability also strengthens resilience against market volatility. Brands that build strong relationships with stakeholders, including conscious consumers, suppliers, and communities, are better positioned to weather disruptions. For instance, ethical sourcing and diversified supply chains mitigate risks related to environmental shocks, social unrest, or reputational crises. Resilient brands maintain continuity and customer trust, giving them a competitive edge during periods of uncertainty.

Marketing and storytelling amplify competitive advantage by articulating the brand's sustainable mission. In crowded markets, brands that can communicate a clear, authentic purpose resonate more strongly with consumers. Narrative-driven marketing that highlights measurable impact, ethical practices, and social contributions differentiates the brand, strengthens emotional connection, and reinforces preference over competitors lacking comparable stories.

Consumer advocacy further extends advantage. Loyal customers of sustainable brands often act as brand ambassadors, promoting the company's ethical practices and influencing peers. Word-of-mouth advocacy in both physical and digital channels amplifies reach without proportional marketing spend, providing a cost-effective way to strengthen market position.

Strategic partnerships and collaborations can also reinforce advantage. Sustainable brands often collaborate with NGOs, social enterprises, or environmental organizations to co-create solutions and expand impact. Such partnerships enhance credibility, increase visibility, and generate shared value, differentiating the brand in a way competitors may struggle to replicate.

Finally, sustainable competitive advantage is increasingly measured by the alignment between corporate actions and societal expectations. Brands that authentically integrate sustainability into their core strategy are better equipped to anticipate trends, adapt to evolving consumer priorities, and maintain relevance. This proactive approach positions them ahead of competitors who treat sustainability as a superficial or reactive initiative.

# Building a Purpose-Driven Brand

# Defining Authentic Brand Purpose

Defining authentic brand purpose is a foundational element of modern marketing, particularly in an era where consumers, employees, and investors increasingly prioritize values alongside products and services. A brand purpose goes beyond functional offerings or profit generation; it articulates why a company exists, the positive impact it seeks to create in the world, and the principles guiding its decisions. When defined authentically, brand purpose becomes a guiding compass that shapes strategy, operations, communications, and stakeholder engagement, creating both tangible and intangible value over the long term.

Authenticity is the cornerstone of an effective brand purpose. It is not enough for a brand to craft a purpose statement that aligns with popular trends or consumer expectations. Authenticity requires that the purpose reflects the company's genuine values, history, capabilities, and strategic priorities. Brands that fail to demonstrate authenticity risk being perceived as opportunistic or insincere, which can erode trust, loyalty, and credibility. Conversely, a purpose rooted in genuine intention resonates with stakeholders, inspires action, and differentiates the brand in a crowded market.

The process of defining authentic brand purpose begins with introspection and alignment. Organizations must examine their origins, culture, mission, and unique competencies to identify the areas where they can create meaningful impact. This involves asking fundamental questions: Why does the company exist beyond making a profit? What societal, environmental, or cultural challenges is the brand uniquely positioned to address? How do its products, services, or operations contribute to a better world? Answering these questions with honesty ensures that the purpose is not superficial but grounded in the brand's reality.

Stakeholder engagement is critical in shaping an authentic purpose. Customers, employees, investors, partners, and communities provide valuable perspectives on what matters, where the brand can make a difference, and how it is perceived in practice. Purpose that is informed by stakeholder insights is more likely to be relevant, credible, and actionable. Listening to these groups also fosters a sense of inclusion and co-creation, reinforcing loyalty and trust.

Authentic brand purpose is closely intertwined with sustainability and corporate responsibility. A purpose that incorporates environmental stewardship, social equity, and ethical governance communicates a commitment to long-term societal impact rather than short-term gain. Brands that align purpose with measurable action—such as reducing carbon emissions, sourcing ethically, or supporting community development—demonstrate credibility and reinforce stakeholder confidence. Purpose without action risks being perceived as marketing rhetoric.

Clarity and simplicity are important in articulating purpose. An authentic brand purpose should be easily understood, memorable, and actionable. It must connect abstract ideals with concrete behaviors and outcomes, ensuring that employees, partners, and consumers can see how it translates into decisions, products, and services. Clear purpose statements serve as a reference point for strategic planning, operational decisions, and marketing communications, ensuring consistency across all touchpoints.

Purpose-driven brands also integrate their mission into internal culture and employee engagement. Authentic purpose inspires employees by providing meaning, aligning personal values with organizational goals, and fostering a sense of contribution beyond financial reward. Engaged employees become ambassadors for the purpose, reinforcing its visibility and credibility in the marketplace. Purpose thus becomes a tool for recruitment, retention, and performance enhancement.

Measurement and accountability are essential to ensure that brand purpose is not only aspirational but operational. Brands must track progress against sustainability initiatives, social impact programs, and ethical commitments to validate that their purpose is creating tangible outcomes. Transparent reporting on achievements and challenges reinforces credibility, builds trust, and strengthens stakeholder relationships. Authentic purpose is demonstrated through consistent action, not merely through statements or campaigns.

An authentic brand purpose also provides differentiation in competitive markets. While products, pricing, and convenience can be easily replicated, purpose-driven differentiation is harder to copy. Brands that genuinely commit to a meaningful cause resonate on an emotional level, fostering loyalty and advocacy among conscious consumers. Purpose adds depth to the brand narrative, creating a long-lasting connection that transcends transactional interactions.

Finally, defining authentic brand purpose requires long-term commitment. Purpose is not static; it must evolve alongside societal expectations, stakeholder priorities, and environmental realities. However, evolution should not compromise authenticity; rather, it reflects a brand's responsiveness, learning, and dedication to sustained impact. Brands that demonstrate consistent alignment between stated purpose and observable action build enduring trust, reputation, and influence.

## Aligning Mission, Vision, and Values

Aligning mission, vision, and values is a critical strategic exercise that ensures organizational coherence, authenticity, and long-term sustainability. While each of these elements—mission, vision, and values—serves a distinct purpose, their alignment creates a strong foundation for decision-making, brand identity, stakeholder trust, and sustainable business performance. Misalignment, on the other hand, can generate confusion, undermine credibility, and erode both internal and external confidence in the organization.

The mission defines the organization's core purpose: why it exists, what it seeks to achieve, and for whom. It is the actionable expression of a company's reason for being and provides guidance for day-to-day operations and strategic initiatives. The vision, by contrast, articulates a future-oriented aspiration: what the organization aims to become or accomplish over the long term. Vision inspires stakeholders by providing direction and ambition, serving as a motivating force that aligns employees and external audiences toward a common goal. Values represent the principles and standards guiding behavior, decision-making, and corporate culture. They embody the ethical, social, and operational norms that shape how the mission is executed and how the vision is pursued.

Alignment among these three elements ensures consistency in purpose, action, and communication. When the mission clearly reflects the organization's true purpose, the vision articulates a meaningful and achievable aspiration, and the values underpin behaviors that bring both to life, stakeholders perceive the brand as credible and authentic. This coherence is particularly important in the context of sustainability and conscious consumer markets, where consumers, investors, and employees scrutinize whether a brand "walks the talk."

Mission-vision alignment provides strategic clarity. The mission grounds the organization in its current purpose, while the vision projects the desired future state. When aligned, strategic initiatives and operational priorities flow naturally from both, reducing conflict, duplication, and inefficiency. For example, a brand whose mission is to provide affordable renewable energy and whose vision is to make clean energy accessible globally will align its investments, partnerships, and innovation efforts to achieve this trajectory. Misalignment between mission and vision can create ambiguity, misguide resource allocation, and dilute strategic impact.

Values play a critical role in translating mission and vision into tangible behaviors. They serve as guiding principles for decision-making, shaping how employees interact with customers, partners, and communities. Values ensure that actions taken in pursuit of mission and vision are ethically grounded and socially responsible. For instance, if a company values transparency and environmental stewardship, its sustainability initiatives and reporting will reflect those commitments, reinforcing authenticity and trust. Misalignment between stated values and operational behavior can lead to perceptions of hypocrisy, undermining credibility and stakeholder confidence.

Aligned mission, vision, and values also strengthen brand identity and differentiation. In crowded markets, consumers are increasingly drawn to brands that demonstrate purpose, consistency, and integrity. When a brand's mission articulates a meaningful reason for existence, its vision outlines a compelling future, and its values guide actions, it creates a coherent narrative that resonates with conscious consumers. This alignment fosters loyalty, advocacy, and preference over competitors who may lack clear or authentic positioning.

Internal engagement and organizational culture benefit significantly from this alignment. Employees understand not only what the organization seeks to achieve, but why it exists and how it expects them to act. This clarity drives motivation, cohesion, and accountability, enabling staff to make decisions consistent with both strategic objectives and ethical principles. Aligned mission, vision, and values also support recruitment, retention, and employee satisfaction, particularly among purpose-driven talent who seek meaningful work and alignment with personal values.

Strategic decision-making is enhanced when these elements are aligned. Every investment, partnership, product launch, or marketing campaign can be evaluated against the organization's mission, vision, and values. This provides a clear framework for prioritization, reduces risk of missteps, and ensures that actions contribute to both long-term goals and ethical standards. In sustainability-focused brands, this alignment ensures that environmental, social, and governance initiatives are not peripheral, but integrated into the core business strategy.

Alignment also builds resilience and adaptability. Organizations that clearly understand their purpose, long-term aspirations, and guiding principles are better equipped to respond to market disruption, regulatory changes, or social shifts. Decisions can be made consistently and confidently, reducing operational uncertainty and enhancing stakeholder trust. In contrast, misaligned mission, vision, and values may result in reactive strategies, fragmented efforts, and reputational vulnerability.

Transparency and communication are essential in maintaining alignment. Stakeholders—customers, employees, investors, and partners—must clearly understand the organization's purpose, ambitions, and principles. Consistent messaging across marketing, reporting, and public engagement reinforces authenticity and credibility. Misalignment between internal culture and external communication can lead to skepticism and erosion of trust.

Measurement and accountability further reinforce alignment. Organizations should track whether strategic initiatives, operational performance, and stakeholder engagement reflect the stated mission, vision, and values. Regular assessment enables course correction, ensures consistency, and demonstrates a commitment to authentic purpose. This practice is particularly important in sustainability-focused organizations, where stakeholders expect tangible outcomes that reflect ethical and environmental commitments.

Finally, aligned mission, vision, and values foster long-term competitive advantage. They create a coherent identity that differentiates the brand, inspires loyalty, guides decision-making, and attracts purpose-driven talent and investment. Alignment ensures that sustainability, social responsibility, and ethical practices are not peripheral initiatives but core elements of strategy that generate enduring value.

## Leadership's Role in Purpose Execution

Leadership's role in purpose execution is critical to transforming a brand's stated mission, vision, and values into tangible impact. While defining purpose is a strategic starting point, its successful implementation depends heavily on leadership's ability to champion, operationalize, and sustain it across the organization. Leaders act as the bridge between abstract ideals and practical action, ensuring that purpose is embedded in strategy, culture, and stakeholder engagement, rather than remaining a symbolic or aspirational statement.

At the core of purpose execution is alignment. Leaders must ensure that organizational strategy, processes, and resources are oriented toward realizing the brand's purpose. This requires translating abstract purpose statements into actionable initiatives, setting measurable goals, and integrating sustainability and ethical considerations into every aspect of decision-making. For example, a brand committed to environmental stewardship must see leadership prioritize eco-friendly supply chains, product design, and operations, ensuring that purpose informs concrete business choices.

Leadership visibility and advocacy are essential. Employees, partners, and stakeholders look to leaders for cues about priorities and expectations. When executives consistently communicate purpose, model ethical behavior, and make decisions reflecting core values, it reinforces the importance of purpose throughout the organization. Leaders who embody the purpose inspire employees, cultivate trust, and establish credibility externally. Conversely, leadership that fails to demonstrate commitment risks creating cynicism, disengagement, and reputational damage.

Decision-making guided by purpose is another critical aspect. Leaders must evaluate strategic choices not only through financial or operational lenses but also through their alignment with ethical, social, and environmental objectives. This might involve trade-offs, such as foregoing short-term profits in favor of long-term societal impact, investing in sustainable innovation, or prioritizing employee well-being over cost minimization. Purpose-driven leadership ensures that such decisions are coherent, consistent, and visibly aligned with the brand's stated mission and values.

Culture-building is a central responsibility of leadership in purpose execution. Leaders shape organizational culture by embedding purpose into policies, practices, and everyday behaviors. They must create an environment where employees understand, embrace, and act in accordance with the brand's purpose. This includes recruitment strategies that prioritize alignment with values, performance management systems that reward ethical behavior, and communication practices that reinforce purpose-driven narratives. A culture grounded in purpose enhances engagement, productivity, and loyalty, both internally and externally.

Measurement and accountability fall squarely under leadership's purview. Leaders must establish clear metrics to assess the organization's progress in realizing its purpose, including social, environmental, and ethical performance indicators. Regular monitoring, transparent reporting, and course correction ensure that purpose is not static rhetoric but a dynamic, evolving part of the organization. Leaders who hold themselves and their teams accountable reinforce credibility and demonstrate that purpose drives real outcomes.

Stakeholder engagement is another critical domain of leadership in purpose execution. Leaders must communicate purpose effectively to investors, consumers, communities, regulators, and partners. This involves articulating tangible initiatives, sharing progress, and addressing challenges openly. Purpose-driven leadership in stakeholder engagement builds trust, strengthens reputation, and positions the brand as authentic and responsible in the marketplace.

Leadership also drives innovation in purpose execution. Purpose-oriented leaders encourage experimentation and creativity to develop solutions that advance social, environmental, or ethical goals. This includes investing in sustainable products, circular business models, or community-focused programs. By fostering innovation aligned with purpose, leaders help the organization differentiate itself in competitive markets and generate both societal and financial value.

Risk management is another area where leadership's role is pivotal. Purpose execution involves anticipating and mitigating risks related to environmental, social, or governance factors. Leaders must integrate ESG considerations into enterprise risk frameworks, proactively identify vulnerabilities, and implement strategies that protect the organization while advancing purpose-driven objectives. Effective risk management ensures that purpose is sustainable, resilient, and credible.

Communication consistency is essential. Leaders must ensure that messaging about purpose is consistent across all levels and touchpoints—internal communications, marketing campaigns, investor reports, and public statements. Inconsistencies between words and actions can undermine trust and weaken the organization's credibility. Leaders who communicate authentically reinforce alignment between purpose and operational reality, strengthening stakeholder confidence.

Leadership succession planning also plays a role in sustaining purpose over time. To maintain continuity, organizations must ensure that future leaders understand, embrace, and are committed to the brand's purpose. Embedding purpose into leadership development programs ensures that organizational values are preserved and evolved, preventing drift or dilution of ethical and sustainability commitments.

Finally, leadership sets the tone for long-term perspective in purpose execution. Purpose-driven initiatives often require time, investment, and patience before yielding measurable impact. Leaders must maintain commitment, navigate short-term pressures, and balance financial performance with societal outcomes. Sustained executive commitment signals to employees, investors, and consumers that purpose is a genuine, integral part of the organization rather than a temporary marketing initiative.

## Internal Culture and Employee Advocacy

**Internal Culture and Employee Advocacy** are pivotal in translating a brand's sustainability commitments and purpose into tangible outcomes. While external communications and marketing strategies often receive the spotlight, the internal culture of an organization—its shared norms, values, and behaviors—directly shapes how sustainability initiatives are executed and perceived. Employees are not just implementers of strategy; they are brand ambassadors whose advocacy amplifies authenticity, builds trust, and strengthens customer and stakeholder engagement.

**Internal culture** refers to the collective mindset, behaviors, and practices that guide how employees interact, make decisions, and approach their work. In a purpose-driven organization, internal culture aligns employees around shared values, ethical principles, and sustainability objectives. It fosters an environment where conscious decision-making, innovation, and responsible behavior are encouraged and rewarded. Culture shapes not only the execution of sustainability initiatives but also how employees perceive their role in creating meaningful impact, which directly influences engagement, retention, and productivity.

A strong sustainability-focused culture begins with leadership modeling the behaviors and priorities they expect throughout the organization. When leaders demonstrate authentic commitment—through decisions, communication, and actions—they set the tone for employees, signaling that sustainability is not optional or symbolic, but integral to business strategy. Leadership that prioritizes purpose and values reinforces an internal culture where ethical, social, and environmental considerations are embedded in everyday operations.

Employee engagement is both a product and a driver of this culture. Employees who understand and connect with the brand's mission and sustainability objectives are more likely to take initiative, suggest improvements, and contribute to innovation. Engagement fosters a sense of ownership and pride, motivating employees to go beyond their defined roles and advocate for the brand's values externally. This engagement becomes a multiplier effect: employees who are inspired internally naturally become authentic advocates externally.

**Employee advocacy** refers to employees actively promoting and defending the brand, its products, and its values to external audiences. In a conscious consumer world, employee advocacy carries significant credibility because it is perceived as authentic, firsthand testimony. Customers, investors, and partners are more likely to trust messages that reflect genuine employee experiences rather than polished marketing campaigns. Advocacy also amplifies sustainability initiatives, raising awareness of ethical practices, community impact, and environmental stewardship.

Creating a culture that encourages advocacy requires investment in education, transparency, and communication. Employees must understand not only the brand's sustainability goals but also the rationale, processes, and measurable outcomes behind these initiatives. When employees are equipped with knowledge, they can confidently communicate the brand's purpose and impact. This empowerment transforms employees into credible storytellers who extend the brand's reach in ways traditional marketing cannot replicate.

Recognition and reward systems are critical in reinforcing both culture and advocacy. Organizations that celebrate employees' contributions to sustainability initiatives and ethical behavior strengthen alignment with brand purpose. Incentives—whether formal awards, professional development opportunities, or public acknowledgment—signal that advocacy and responsible action are valued, further embedding sustainability into the organizational DNA.

Culture and advocacy also drive innovation. Employees embedded in a purpose-driven environment are more likely to propose creative solutions to sustainability challenges, identify efficiency gains, or design socially responsible products and services. This internal engagement generates both operational benefits and differentiation in competitive markets. When employees see their input influencing tangible outcomes, advocacy becomes more authentic, and culture strengthens in a positive feedback loop.

Moreover, internal culture shapes resilience and consistency. Purpose-driven organizations with strong internal alignment are better equipped to maintain standards during crises, operational disruptions, or market pressures. Employees who internalize the brand's values and sustainability commitments are more likely to act responsibly under stress, protect the company's reputation, and reinforce consistent messaging externally.

Cross-functional integration of culture ensures that advocacy is not limited to specific departments but permeates all aspects of the organization—from R&D and operations to sales, marketing, and customer service. This holistic approach ensures that sustainability principles are embedded into decision-making at every level, creating a coherent brand experience for stakeholders.

Finally, internal culture and employee advocacy together enhance long-term brand credibility and trust. When sustainability is visibly lived within the organization, and employees actively champion these initiatives externally, stakeholders perceive the brand as authentic and reliable. This strengthens customer loyalty, investor confidence, and overall brand equity. In a crowded, conscious-consumer-driven marketplace, the alignment of culture and advocacy becomes a competitive differentiator that reinforces both purpose and performance.

## Avoiding Purpose Dilution and Inconsistency

**Avoiding Purpose Dilution and Inconsistency** is essential for sustaining credibility, trust, and long-term impact in a purpose-driven brand. In today's conscious consumer world, stakeholders—customers, employees, investors, and partners—scrutinize whether a brand's stated purpose aligns with its actions. Any misalignment, superficial engagement, or contradictory messaging can dilute the brand's purpose, reduce authenticity, and erode both loyalty and market position. Purpose must therefore be consistently integrated into every aspect of the organization to avoid perception gaps that undermine credibility.

**Purpose dilution** occurs when a brand's mission or values are weakened by conflicting actions, inconsistent messaging, or superficial initiatives. For example, a company that claims to prioritize environmental sustainability but engages in practices that generate significant carbon emissions or fails to maintain ethical supply chains risks being perceived as insincere. Even minor inconsistencies can create skepticism among stakeholders, especially in an age of transparency where information is readily accessible.

Brands that dilute purpose risk not only losing consumer trust but also diminishing employee engagement, investor confidence, and overall brand equity.

Inconsistency can arise across multiple dimensions—strategy, operations, communications, and partnerships. Strategically, purpose must inform decision-making at every level. Decisions that prioritize short-term financial gain over the brand's mission can signal misalignment. Operationally, all processes, products, and supply chains must reflect the stated purpose. For example, a brand promoting fair labor practices must ensure compliance across all suppliers and contractors; any deviation can damage credibility. Communication inconsistency—such as marketing messages that exaggerate impact or fail to reflect actual practices—further undermines authenticity. Partnerships and collaborations also matter; associations with organizations that contradict the brand's stated purpose can create dissonance and stakeholder doubt.

Avoiding purpose dilution requires **clarity and focus**. Brands must clearly define their purpose, identify priorities, and communicate boundaries. A purpose that is too broad or generic risks becoming meaningless or easily contradicted by day-to-day decisions. Focused purpose enables organizations to align initiatives, measure progress effectively, and consistently convey their impact, thereby reinforcing stakeholder confidence.

Leadership plays a pivotal role in maintaining purpose integrity. Executives and managers must model behavior, make decisions aligned with purpose, and hold teams accountable for consistency. Leadership commitment ensures that purpose is not treated as a marketing slogan but as a guiding principle shaping culture, operations, and strategic choices. When leadership demonstrates alignment between words and actions, it reinforces internal and external trust, reducing the risk of purpose dilution.

Employee engagement and culture are equally important. Employees must understand the brand's purpose, see how it connects to their work, and feel empowered to act in alignment with it. Training, internal communication, and performance metrics tied to purpose help ensure consistent behavior and decision-making across the organization. When employees internalize purpose, they become authentic advocates, reinforcing consistency externally through customer interactions, social media, and community engagement.

Transparent measurement and reporting help prevent both dilution and inconsistency. By tracking progress against sustainability, ethical, and social goals, brands can validate that their purpose is producing measurable outcomes. Public disclosure of achievements and challenges builds credibility and demonstrates accountability, reducing perceptions of superficiality. Metrics should cover both quantitative impact (e.g., emissions reduction, social program reach) and qualitative alignment (e.g., stakeholder perceptions, ethical compliance).

Communication consistency is critical. All external messaging—advertising, PR, social media, and investor reports—must reflect the same purpose-driven narrative. Contradictory or exaggerated messaging can rapidly undermine trust, particularly in the age of digital scrutiny and conscious consumer activism. Purpose must also be consistently communicated internally, reinforcing alignment between organizational strategy and employee behavior.

Strategic integration across the value chain is another mechanism to prevent dilution. Purpose should inform procurement, production, logistics, marketing, and customer experience. For instance, a sustainability-focused brand must ensure eco-friendly sourcing, packaging, distribution, and after-sales service. Any disconnect along the value chain can create perception gaps and weaken authenticity.

Finally, brands must remain vigilant against external pressures that encourage short-term compromise. Market volatility, competitive pressure, or immediate financial incentives may tempt organizations to prioritize short-term gains over purpose-aligned actions. Purpose integrity requires disciplined decision-making that resists such compromises and prioritizes long-term alignment with the brand's mission, vision, and values.

# Sustainable Product and Service Design

# Lifecycle Thinking and Circular Design

**Lifecycle Thinking and Circular Design** are fundamental concepts in sustainable marketing and product development, offering brands a framework to minimize environmental impact, optimize resource use, and deliver long-term value. These approaches shift the focus from linear "take-make-dispose" models toward regenerative, closed-loop systems that consider a product's entire journey—from raw material sourcing to end-of-life management—thereby reinforcing a brand's sustainability commitments and credibility.

**Lifecycle thinking** is a holistic approach that examines the environmental, social, and economic impacts of a product or service at every stage of its existence. This begins with raw material extraction, continues through manufacturing, distribution, use, and maintenance, and concludes with disposal, recycling, or repurposing. By evaluating the entire lifecycle, brands can identify areas where energy consumption, emissions, waste, and social impact can be reduced. This perspective encourages proactive decision-making, ensuring that sustainability is integrated into all phases rather than addressed as an afterthought.

Lifecycle thinking encourages brands to ask critical questions: Are raw materials sourced responsibly? Can manufacturing processes be optimized for efficiency or lower emissions? Are products designed for durability, repairability, or recyclability? How can logistics minimize carbon footprint? What happens to the product at the end of its useful life? Addressing these questions holistically enables brands to reduce environmental impact, enhance operational efficiency, and communicate authentic sustainability claims to conscious consumers.

**Circular design** complements lifecycle thinking by embedding principles of reuse, repair, refurbishment, and recycling into product development. Unlike traditional linear models, circular design seeks to extend the useful life of materials and products, keeping them in circulation rather than allowing them to become waste. This includes designing products that are modular, durable, or easily disassembled, and creating business models that support take-back programs, refurbishing, and resource recovery. Circular design turns potential waste into value, aligning economic performance with environmental responsibility.

One critical advantage of circular design is its potential to reduce material dependency and operational risk. By designing for reuse or recyclability, companies decrease reliance on virgin resources, reduce exposure to raw material price volatility, and mitigate supply chain vulnerabilities. Circular approaches also foster innovation, as teams explore new materials, business models, and processes to create regenerative value. This not only strengthens sustainability credentials but can also create differentiation in competitive markets.

Lifecycle thinking and circular design also enhance transparency and accountability in sustainability reporting. Brands that can quantify environmental impact across the product lifecycle and demonstrate circularity initiatives are better positioned to communicate authentic, measurable achievements to consumers, investors, and regulators. This transparency reinforces trust and strengthens brand equity, particularly in markets where conscious consumers scrutinize green claims.

Consumer engagement is another key dimension. Circular design can empower consumers to participate in sustainability initiatives through product return programs, recycling schemes, or modular product upgrades. Lifecycle thinking informs educational communication that helps consumers understand the environmental impact of their choices and the benefits of participating in circular systems. Engaged consumers become advocates, amplifying the brand's purpose-driven narrative.

Operational integration is essential for both lifecycle thinking and circular design to succeed. Cross-functional collaboration between R&D, procurement, manufacturing, marketing, and supply chain teams ensures that sustainability principles are embedded in product strategy, design specifications, and service offerings. This alignment transforms sustainability from a compliance or marketing function into a core organizational competency.

Economic benefits further reinforce the business case for these approaches. Reducing material use, improving resource efficiency, and enabling product longevity can lower costs, increase profitability, and open new revenue streams through refurbished products, leasing models, or secondary markets. Brands that integrate circular principles can achieve competitive advantage while demonstrating meaningful social and environmental impact.

Moreover, lifecycle thinking and circular design support regulatory compliance and risk mitigation. Governments and industry bodies increasingly set standards for product sustainability, emissions, and waste management. Brands that incorporate these practices proactively reduce regulatory risk, avoid penalties, and strengthen their license to operate globally.

Finally, integrating lifecycle thinking and circular design contributes to long-term brand purpose and authenticity. Brands that design products and systems with sustainability in mind demonstrate a commitment to ethical practices, environmental stewardship, and social responsibility. This alignment with conscious consumer values fosters loyalty, enhances brand equity, and reinforces the organization's credibility in a crowded, purpose-driven market.

## Responsible Sourcing and Supply Chains

**Responsible Sourcing and Supply Chains** are critical pillars in building sustainable brands and ensuring credibility in a conscious consumer world. As organizations face increasing scrutiny from customers, investors, regulators, and communities, the integrity and ethics of sourcing practices and supply chain operations have become as important as product quality or pricing. Responsible sourcing is not merely about acquiring materials—it encompasses environmental stewardship, ethical labor practices, transparency, and long-term social impact across every tier of the supply chain.

At its core, **responsible sourcing** involves procuring raw materials, components, and services in ways that minimize negative environmental and social impacts while maximizing positive contributions to communities and ecosystems. This includes sourcing from suppliers who adhere to fair labor standards, respect human rights, minimize ecological damage, and comply with applicable laws and industry standards. Ethical sourcing also considers long-term partnerships that promote mutual benefit, social development, and resilience, rather than opportunistic, short-term cost reduction.

Supply chains are often complex, spanning multiple geographies, industries, and layers of subcontracting. Without careful oversight, brands risk exposure to unethical practices such as forced labor, unsafe working conditions, or environmental degradation. Responsible supply chain management emphasizes transparency and accountability, ensuring that all suppliers, partners, and intermediaries comply with the brand's sustainability standards. By conducting audits, certifications, and risk assessments, companies can identify vulnerabilities and implement corrective measures before they escalate into reputational or operational crises.

**Environmental considerations** in sourcing and supply chains are equally critical. Sustainable brands prioritize renewable, recycled, or low-impact materials; reduce energy consumption in production and logistics; and minimize waste and carbon emissions. This approach not only addresses climate concerns but also builds operational resilience against resource scarcity and regulatory pressures. For instance, sourcing responsibly from certified forestry or agricultural programs ensures both legal compliance and long-term ecosystem health.

**Social responsibility** is another key dimension. Responsible sourcing ensures fair wages, safe working conditions, and community development for workers across the supply chain. Brands that actively engage with suppliers to improve social conditions demonstrate ethical leadership and strengthen trust with stakeholders. Ethical labor practices reduce risk, enhance productivity, and contribute to the brand's reputation as a responsible corporate citizen.

**Transparency and traceability** are fundamental to responsible sourcing. Consumers and investors increasingly demand clear evidence that brands' claims about sustainability and ethics are valid. This requires accurate reporting and visibility into sourcing practices, from raw materials to finished goods. Tools such as blockchain, digital tracking systems, and supplier scorecards help organizations maintain accountability, validate compliance, and communicate credibility externally. Transparency also allows brands to respond proactively to challenges or crises, mitigating reputational damage.

**Collaboration with suppliers** is essential for long-term impact. Brands must work with suppliers to build capacity, share best practices, and support sustainable innovation. Collaborative relationships foster trust, create incentives for compliance, and enable systemic improvements in labor practices, environmental management, and operational efficiency. This approach transforms supply chains from a transactional focus to a partnership model, where mutual growth and sustainability are prioritized.

**Risk management** is a critical aspect of responsible sourcing. Ethical, environmental, and operational risks can arise at any point in the supply chain, including geopolitical instability, labor disputes, resource scarcity, and regulatory non-compliance. By proactively assessing and mitigating these risks, brands protect their reputation, ensure continuity of supply, and align with stakeholder expectations. Companies that fail to address supply chain risks may face financial penalties, negative publicity, or loss of consumer trust.

**Regulatory compliance and industry standards** further guide responsible sourcing. Increasingly, governments and international organizations mandate environmental, social, and governance standards for global supply chains. Brands adhering to recognized certifications—such as Fair Trade, Rainforest Alliance, ISO standards, or Conflict-Free sourcing—demonstrate compliance and reinforce credibility. Aligning sourcing practices with regulatory frameworks also prepares brands for future policy changes and reduces operational disruptions.

**Consumer engagement** is enhanced by responsible sourcing. Modern consumers, especially Millennials and Gen Z, actively seek products that align with their values, including ethical sourcing and sustainable practices. Brands that communicate their supply chain integrity effectively can strengthen loyalty, differentiate themselves in competitive markets, and justify premium pricing. Transparency about sourcing practices becomes a storytelling tool that reinforces brand purpose and builds emotional connection with consumers.

Finally, responsible sourcing and supply chain management are inseparable from long-term brand strategy. By embedding sustainability into sourcing decisions, operational policies, and supplier relationships, brands create resilient, transparent, and purpose-driven systems that support both social and environmental impact while driving financial performance. Ethical, sustainable supply chains are not just a compliance necessity—they are a strategic lever for competitive advantage, stakeholder trust, and lasting brand equity.

## Eco-Innovation and Material Choices

**Eco-Innovation and Material Choices** are critical drivers of sustainability in product development, brand differentiation, and long-term value creation. Eco-innovation refers to the development of products, services, processes, or business models that reduce environmental impact while delivering functional or economic benefits. Material choices, as a core component of eco-innovation, influence the environmental footprint, resource efficiency, durability, and overall sustainability of a product. Together, these elements enable brands to respond to conscious consumer expectations, regulatory pressures, and competitive differentiation in a crowded marketplace.

At its core, **eco-innovation** emphasizes creating solutions that are both environmentally responsible and economically viable. It goes beyond incremental improvements to traditional products and processes, encouraging radical or systemic change that reduces resource consumption, energy use, and waste generation. Eco-innovation can include lightweight or energy-efficient product designs, closed-loop manufacturing systems, renewable energy integration, water-saving production processes, and digital tools that optimize supply chains. By adopting eco-innovation, brands signal purpose-driven leadership and commitment to sustainable practices, enhancing credibility among conscious consumers and investors.

**Material choices** are central to eco-innovation because they determine the ecological impact of the product from its origin to end-of-life. Sustainable materials include renewable resources, recycled content, biodegradable options, and low-impact synthetics that reduce carbon emissions, pollution, and resource depletion. Selecting appropriate materials also involves considering durability, repairability, and recyclability, ensuring that the product's lifecycle aligns with circular economy principles. For example, using recycled aluminum or responsibly sourced wood not only minimizes environmental impact but also communicates a tangible commitment to sustainability.

The selection of materials also intersects with **health and safety considerations**. Eco-friendly materials often reduce exposure to harmful chemicals, toxins, or allergens, benefiting both consumers and workers in the supply chain. Brands that prioritize safe and sustainable materials enhance trust, comply with regulatory standards, and differentiate themselves in markets where ethical and environmental responsibility are increasingly valued.

**Innovation in material science** is a key enabler of eco-innovation. Emerging technologies allow brands to create high-performance materials that are sustainable yet functional. Examples include bio-based plastics, plant-derived textiles, low-carbon cement alternatives, and advanced composites with recycled content. These innovations enable brands to deliver quality, performance, and sustainability simultaneously, addressing one of the traditional trade-offs between environmental responsibility and product effectiveness.

Eco-innovation and material choices also support **lifecycle thinking**. Brands that evaluate the environmental impact of materials across extraction, processing, manufacturing, use, and disposal can make informed decisions that reduce carbon footprints, minimize waste, and support circularity. Material selection impacts energy use in production, transportation efficiency, and recyclability at the end of life. Aligning material choices with lifecycle principles ensures that sustainability is integrated into every stage of the product journey.

Consumer perception is significantly influenced by eco-innovation and material choices. Conscious consumers increasingly demand transparency about what goes into products, how they are made, and their environmental implications. Brands that communicate responsible material choices, innovative sustainable features, or energy-efficient designs reinforce trust and brand loyalty. Packaging, labeling, and marketing materials that highlight eco-innovative attributes amplify the impact of these choices on consumer perception and preference.

Operational efficiency is another benefit. Sustainable material choices can reduce costs associated with waste management, energy consumption, or regulatory compliance. For example, lightweight or renewable materials can lower transportation costs and emissions, while durable materials reduce returns or replacements. Eco-innovation often drives efficiency across the value chain, creating both environmental and economic advantages.

**Collaboration and partnerships** play a crucial role in advancing eco-innovation. Brands often work with material scientists, suppliers, research institutions, or startups to identify novel materials and develop scalable sustainable solutions. These partnerships facilitate knowledge sharing, technological advancement, and faster adoption of environmentally responsible practices. Collaborative innovation strengthens credibility and positions brands as leaders in sustainable development.

Finally, eco-innovation and material choices are inseparable from long-term brand purpose. They demonstrate a tangible commitment to sustainability, operational integrity, and ethical responsibility. Brands that embed eco-innovation into product design and material selection build resilience, respond proactively to regulatory trends, and meet the expectations of conscious consumers who value authenticity and impact.

## Sustainable Packaging and Logistics

**Sustainable Packaging and Logistics** are critical components of a brand's sustainability strategy, directly influencing environmental impact, operational efficiency, and stakeholder perception. As conscious consumers increasingly scrutinize the lifecycle of products, packaging and distribution practices have become central to a brand's credibility and differentiation. Sustainable packaging reduces waste, minimizes carbon footprint, and aligns with ethical consumption values, while sustainable logistics ensures efficient, low-impact transportation and distribution throughout the supply chain.

**Sustainable packaging** involves designing and using materials that minimize environmental harm while maintaining product protection, functionality, and appeal. This includes reducing material usage, selecting recyclable, biodegradable, or compostable materials, and employing innovative designs that maximize efficiency. Lightweight packaging, modular containers, and refillable or reusable systems are examples of approaches that decrease resource consumption and environmental impact. By prioritizing sustainable materials and designs, brands not only demonstrate environmental stewardship but also respond to consumer demand for eco-friendly alternatives.

Packaging also communicates purpose and brand values. Thoughtfully designed, sustainable packaging reinforces a brand's commitment to environmental responsibility and ethical practices. Clear labeling, transparent material sourcing, and messaging about recyclability or carbon footprint educate consumers, empower informed choices, and strengthen emotional connection with the brand. Packaging thus becomes both a functional necessity and a storytelling tool that supports brand authenticity.

**Logistics**, encompassing transportation, warehousing, and distribution, significantly contributes to a product's carbon footprint.

Sustainable logistics seeks to optimize these processes to reduce environmental impact while maintaining efficiency and service quality. Key strategies include route optimization, fuel-efficient vehicles, intermodal transport, load consolidation, and adoption of renewable energy sources in warehouses and distribution centers. By implementing sustainable logistics practices, brands reduce greenhouse gas emissions, energy consumption, and operational costs, creating both environmental and financial benefits.

Integration of sustainable packaging and logistics requires **holistic lifecycle thinking**. Decisions about packaging materials, size, and design influence transportation efficiency, storage space, and energy consumption. Lightweight, stackable, or modular packaging can reduce shipping volume, fuel consumption, and associated emissions. Coordinating packaging and logistics strategies ensures that sustainability gains are maximized across the entire supply chain rather than being isolated initiatives.

Consumer engagement is enhanced through sustainable packaging and logistics. Conscious consumers increasingly expect brands to consider the environmental impact of packaging and delivery. Brands that transparently communicate their sustainable practices, such as carbon-neutral shipping, recyclable packaging, or minimal waste solutions, build trust and loyalty. These practices can also influence purchasing behavior, as consumers are more likely to support companies demonstrating tangible environmental responsibility.

Innovation drives sustainable packaging and logistics. Brands are exploring bio-based materials, plant-derived inks, reusable containers, and packaging that serves secondary purposes, such as storage or utility. In logistics, advancements in electric and hybrid fleets, autonomous delivery systems, and AI-driven route planning optimize efficiency and reduce environmental impact. Continuous innovation ensures that sustainable practices remain competitive and forward-looking.

Collaboration and partnerships are crucial. Working with suppliers, transport providers, and material innovators allows brands to implement scalable, sustainable solutions across the supply chain. Joint initiatives, such as take-back programs, recycling partnerships, or carbon-offset logistics, strengthen credibility, expand impact, and enhance stakeholder perception.

Regulatory compliance and standards further reinforce sustainable packaging and logistics. Many governments and industry bodies are implementing stricter requirements for packaging waste, carbon emissions, and supply chain transparency. Brands that proactively adopt sustainable practices not only mitigate regulatory risks but also position themselves as responsible leaders in their markets.

Operational efficiency is another key benefit. Optimized packaging reduces material costs and waste management expenses, while sustainable logistics minimizes fuel consumption and transportation costs. These efficiencies support profitability while reinforcing environmental responsibility, demonstrating that sustainability and business performance can be mutually reinforcing.

Finally, sustainable packaging and logistics support long-term brand purpose and authenticity. They exemplify actionable steps that translate abstract commitments into visible, measurable impact. Brands that integrate sustainable practices into these operational areas reinforce their ethical positioning, strengthen consumer trust, and differentiate themselves in competitive, conscious-consumer-driven markets.

## Balancing Cost, Performance, and Impact

**Balancing Cost, Performance, and Impact** is a central challenge for organizations striving to integrate sustainability into their products, services, and operations. While conscious consumers and stakeholders increasingly demand environmentally responsible and socially ethical practices, businesses must simultaneously maintain profitability, competitiveness, and operational excellence. Achieving equilibrium among financial cost, product or service performance, and environmental or social impact requires strategic planning, innovation, and rigorous decision-making across the organization.

**Cost considerations** are often the first challenge in sustainability initiatives. Sustainable materials, energy-efficient processes, eco-friendly packaging, and ethical sourcing can carry higher upfront expenses compared to conventional alternatives. These costs may affect production budgets, pricing strategies, and short-term profitability. Organizations must therefore assess the total cost of ownership, including lifecycle savings, operational efficiencies, and long-term reputational benefits, rather than focusing solely on immediate expenditure. Investments in sustainability often deliver returns through reduced resource use, regulatory compliance, energy savings, and stronger brand loyalty, offsetting initial costs over time.

**Performance** encompasses both functional quality and reliability. Products or services must meet or exceed customer expectations while integrating sustainable features. A high-performance product ensures consumer satisfaction, minimizes returns or replacements, and supports brand reputation. Balancing sustainability with performance requires careful selection of materials, process innovation, and design optimization. For example, using recycled materials should not compromise durability, safety, or user experience. Companies that achieve this balance demonstrate that sustainability can coexist with excellence, creating a competitive advantage in the marketplace.

**Impact** refers to environmental, social, and ethical outcomes associated with a product, service, or operation. Brands must consider carbon footprint, water usage, waste generation, ethical labor practices, and broader societal effects. Prioritizing impact often involves trade-offs: certain materials may be environmentally preferable but costlier, or energy-efficient processes may require higher initial investment. Lifecycle assessment and comprehensive sustainability metrics enable organizations to quantify impact and make informed decisions that align with purpose without compromising cost or performance unduly.

Strategic frameworks such as **triple-bottom-line thinking** and **sustainable value mapping** are instrumental in balancing these dimensions. Triple-bottom-line thinking evaluates outcomes across economic, social, and environmental dimensions, helping organizations identify solutions that provide holistic benefits. Sustainable value mapping quantifies trade-offs and synergies between cost, performance, and impact, guiding investment and operational decisions. These approaches enable leaders to make choices that optimize overall value rather than favoring a single dimension.

**Innovation** is a key enabler in achieving balance. Advances in material science, production processes, and design allow brands to reduce environmental impact without sacrificing performance or inflating costs. Examples include lightweight packaging that lowers shipping costs and emissions, energy-efficient manufacturing technologies that reduce operational expenses, and modular product designs that enhance longevity and repairability. By fostering a culture of eco-innovation, organizations can discover solutions that satisfy all three dimensions concurrently.

**Cross-functional collaboration** is essential. Teams across R&D, procurement, operations, marketing, and finance must coordinate to ensure that sustainability objectives align with performance targets and cost constraints. For instance, procurement decisions on sustainable suppliers must consider pricing, quality standards, and ethical credentials, while R&D must design products that optimize material use, durability, and functionality. Integrated planning ensures trade-offs are managed strategically rather than in isolation.

**Consumer perception and willingness to pay** also play a role. Conscious consumers increasingly value sustainability and are willing to pay a premium for products and services that reduce environmental or social impact. Understanding this dynamic allows brands to justify slightly higher costs or invest in eco-innovations that enhance performance and impact. Transparent communication about sustainability benefits helps manage expectations and reinforces perceived value, mitigating concerns about higher pricing.

**Risk management** further reinforces balance. Unsustainable practices can create reputational, regulatory, or operational risks, potentially exceeding cost savings from cheaper or conventional alternatives. Integrating sustainability into supply chains, manufacturing, and product design mitigates these risks while ensuring consistent performance and ethical compliance. Thoughtful investment in sustainable practices can therefore be framed as a risk-avoidance strategy as well as a strategic differentiator.

**Measurement and continuous improvement** are critical. Brands must track cost, performance, and impact metrics, analyzing trade-offs and identifying opportunities to optimize all three. Key performance indicators (KPIs) might include energy consumption per unit produced, material efficiency ratios, customer satisfaction scores, lifecycle emissions, and social impact indices. By regularly evaluating outcomes, organizations can adjust processes, materials, and strategies to achieve a better balance over time.

Finally, aligning cost, performance, and impact reinforces **long-term brand purpose and competitiveness**. Organizations that manage these three dimensions effectively demonstrate authenticity, operational intelligence, and commitment to sustainability. This alignment strengthens stakeholder trust, enhances market positioning, and creates lasting value, proving that sustainability need not come at the expense of profitability or quality.

# Ethical Communication and Storytelling

# Transparency in Marketing Claims

**Transparency in Marketing Claims** is a cornerstone of trust and credibility for purpose-driven and sustainable brands. In a marketplace where conscious consumers increasingly scrutinize brand messaging, transparency ensures that marketing communications are accurate, verifiable, and aligned with the company's actual practices. Without transparency, brands risk being accused of greenwashing or misleading claims, which can severely damage reputation, erode consumer trust, and undermine long-term brand equity.

At its core, transparency in marketing involves **truthful communication** about products, services, and corporate practices. This means providing accurate information on sustainability initiatives, sourcing practices, environmental impact, social responsibility, and ethical standards. Marketing messages should reflect verifiable facts, data, or certifications, avoiding exaggeration or ambiguity that could mislead stakeholders. For example, stating that a product is "eco-friendly" should be supported by measurable criteria, such as recycled content percentage, energy efficiency, or carbon footprint reduction.

**Authenticity** is inseparable from transparency. Consumers can easily detect incongruence between brand claims and actual practices, especially in the age of social media, independent reviews, and third-party verification. Brands that communicate openly about both achievements and challenges demonstrate honesty and build credibility. Acknowledging areas for improvement or ongoing initiatives signals commitment and fosters trust, whereas overstated or unsubstantiated claims can trigger skepticism and backlash.

**Third-party certifications and audits** play a critical role in ensuring transparency. Recognized standards—such as Fair Trade, Rainforest Alliance, ISO, or LEED certifications—provide objective validation of marketing claims. By referencing these certifications in communications, brands strengthen credibility, provide tangible proof of sustainability, and reduce consumer uncertainty.

Transparency is enhanced when brands clearly explain what the certification entails, how compliance is measured, and what impact it achieves.

**Detail and specificity** are essential. Vague or generic claims—such as "green," "natural," or "sustainable"—can confuse consumers or appear superficial. Transparent marketing communicates precise information: the type of materials used, the percentage of recycled content, the energy savings achieved, or the social initiatives supported. Detailed communication educates consumers, empowers informed decisions, and positions the brand as accountable and responsible.

**Consistency across channels** reinforces transparency. Marketing claims should align with product labeling, website content, social media messaging, advertisements, and public reports. Inconsistent messaging can create confusion and damage credibility, even if individual claims are accurate. Integrated communication ensures that all stakeholder touchpoints reflect the same narrative, reinforcing trust and authenticity.

**Stakeholder engagement** enhances transparency. Open dialogue with consumers, employees, investors, and communities allows brands to clarify claims, provide context, and respond to questions or concerns. Social media platforms, feedback mechanisms, and corporate reporting channels are effective tools for fostering accountability and demonstrating responsiveness. Engaging stakeholders not only validates claims but also strengthens brand reputation through participatory transparency.

**Measurement and reporting** are key enablers. Brands should track and publicly report outcomes related to sustainability initiatives, ethical sourcing, and social impact. Metrics such as carbon reduction, energy efficiency, waste diversion, or community investment provide tangible evidence that supports marketing claims. Transparent reporting demonstrates that the brand is committed to measurable progress, rather than symbolic gestures, and allows stakeholders to hold the organization accountable.

**Avoiding greenwashing** is a critical aspect of transparency. Greenwashing occurs when a brand exaggerates or fabricates sustainability claims, creating a misleading perception of environmental or social responsibility. Transparent marketing proactively counters this risk by ensuring that claims are substantiated, contextualized, and aligned with verified practices. Brands that prioritize transparency protect their reputation and maintain consumer confidence in a skeptical and information-rich market.

Transparency also supports **long-term brand value and differentiation**. In a crowded market, brands that consistently provide honest, verifiable information about their sustainability efforts gain consumer loyalty and trust. Transparent marketing fosters emotional connection, reinforces purpose-driven positioning, and creates advocacy, as informed consumers are more likely to recommend and support brands whose claims they trust.

Finally, transparency is an ongoing commitment, not a one-time initiative. Brands must continuously update claims to reflect evolving practices, improvements, and challenges. Dynamic transparency demonstrates accountability, adaptability, and integrity, ensuring that marketing communications remain credible and aligned with actual performance.

## Storytelling Without Greenwashing

**Storytelling Without Greenwashing** is a vital practice for brands aiming to communicate sustainability, social responsibility, and purpose authentically. In an era of conscious consumerism, customers, investors, and other stakeholders are increasingly adept at detecting insincere or exaggerated claims. Storytelling, when done correctly, can inspire, educate, and build emotional connection—but if mishandled, it risks being perceived as greenwashing, which can damage trust, credibility, and long-term brand equity.

At its core, **storytelling without greenwashing** is about communicating a brand's sustainability journey with honesty, clarity, and evidence. Rather than relying on vague claims such as "eco-friendly" or "green," brands must provide concrete examples, measurable results, and transparent context. For instance, instead of stating a product is "sustainable," a brand can share how 60% of its materials are recycled, outline its energy reduction initiatives, or describe community impact programs. The story should connect values to tangible actions, making sustainability relatable and verifiable.

**Authenticity** is central to this approach. Brands must align their narrative with actual practices, avoiding exaggeration, selective reporting, or embellishment. Consumers are quick to identify inconsistencies between marketing messages and real-world behavior, particularly in the age of social media and independent reviews. Authentic storytelling demonstrates that the brand's purpose is embedded in operations, product design, and corporate culture, rather than being a superficial marketing tactic.

**Transparency and evidence** are critical safeguards against greenwashing. Every claim or narrative shared should be supported by data, certifications, audits, or verifiable outcomes. Third-party validation—such as Fair Trade, Rainforest Alliance, or carbon-neutral certifications—provides credibility and reinforces trust. By including measurable impact and acknowledging areas for improvement, brands demonstrate accountability, honesty, and a commitment to continuous progress rather than perfection.

**Narrative structure and context** enhance effective storytelling. A compelling sustainability story combines the "why" (brand purpose and values), the "what" (specific actions and initiatives), and the "how" (processes, challenges, and measurable results). Providing context—such as explaining the environmental challenge being addressed or why certain initiatives were prioritized—helps audiences understand the relevance and authenticity of the brand's efforts. This approach turns sustainability from abstract messaging into a relatable, human-centered story.

**Avoiding selective storytelling** is another key principle. Greenwashing often occurs when brands highlight a single positive action while ignoring broader negative impacts. Storytelling without greenwashing requires acknowledging the complete picture, including challenges, limitations, or areas for improvement. By sharing both successes and ongoing efforts, brands create credibility, demonstrate commitment to learning and evolution, and foster trust with stakeholders.

**Consumer engagement and participatory storytelling** amplify authenticity. Encouraging customers, employees, or community members to share their experiences with sustainability initiatives creates a multi-dimensional narrative. User-generated content, case studies, or interactive campaigns demonstrate real-world impact and allow audiences to verify claims through firsthand experiences, reinforcing credibility and emotional connection.

**Consistency across all channels** is essential. Stories shared in advertising, social media, product packaging, corporate reports, and public communications must align with operational reality. Discrepancies between what a brand claims and what it does create suspicion and undermine the narrative. Integrated communication ensures that every touchpoint reinforces authenticity and strengthens stakeholder trust.

**Leadership and employee involvement** also play a role in storytelling. When executives and employees actively participate in sustainability initiatives and share their experiences, it demonstrates lived commitment. Authentic voices within the organization—rather than solely external marketing teams—enhance credibility and illustrate that sustainability is embedded in the organizational culture.

**Long-term perspective** is crucial. Storytelling without greenwashing focuses on ongoing efforts, evolution, and continuous improvement. Brands that acknowledge progress over time, set future goals, and transparently report results demonstrate commitment to sustainability as a strategic priority rather than a temporary marketing trend. This approach builds loyalty, differentiates the brand, and positions it as a credible leader in a conscious consumer world.

# Data-Backed Sustainability Messaging

**Data-Backed Sustainability Messaging** is a crucial strategy for brands seeking credibility, trust, and impact in a conscious consumer marketplace. While consumers increasingly value sustainability and ethical responsibility, they are also highly skeptical of vague or exaggerated claims. Using accurate, verifiable, and contextualized data allows brands to communicate sustainability initiatives with authority, authenticity, and transparency, differentiating themselves from competitors and reinforcing long-term brand equity.

At its core, data-backed messaging relies on **quantifiable evidence** to support sustainability claims. Rather than using general statements like "we care about the environment" or "our products are eco-friendly," brands provide measurable outcomes—such as carbon emissions reductions, percentage of recycled materials, energy savings, water usage reductions, or community impact metrics. These metrics make claims verifiable and tangible, giving stakeholders confidence that the brand's actions align with its stated purpose.

**Credibility** is a primary advantage of data-driven sustainability communication. Conscious consumers, investors, and regulators increasingly demand proof behind marketing claims. By presenting transparent, accurate, and independently validated data, brands reduce the risk of being perceived as greenwashing. Third-party audits, certifications, and standardized reporting frameworks—such as ISO 14001, B Corp, or CDP (Carbon Disclosure Project)—further reinforce credibility by providing objective validation of claims.

**Specificity and context** enhance the impact of data-backed messaging. Metrics should not only quantify results but also explain their significance. For instance, a brand stating that it reduced packaging waste by 30% can contextualize this achievement by showing how it compares to industry averages, the environmental benefits realized, or the social value created. Contextualized data helps consumers, employees, and investors understand the relevance and real-world impact of sustainability initiatives, strengthening engagement and trust.

**Transparency and disclosure** are essential. Brands should openly share both successes and challenges, providing a balanced view of sustainability performance. Reporting limitations, ongoing projects, or areas for improvement demonstrates honesty and reinforces commitment to continuous progress. Transparent communication builds credibility, even when results are imperfect, because stakeholders recognize a genuine effort to measure, learn, and improve.

**Integration across channels** is critical for effective data-backed messaging. Sustainability metrics and achievements should be communicated consistently across product packaging, marketing campaigns, annual reports, social media, websites, and investor briefings. Inconsistent or selective communication can create confusion or skepticism, while a coherent narrative reinforces authenticity and positions the brand as accountable and transparent.

**Storytelling combined with data** is a powerful tool. While metrics provide credibility, narratives make data relatable and emotionally engaging. For example, a brand reducing water consumption in manufacturing can share stories of communities benefiting from water savings, illustrating both numerical impact and human relevance. By merging quantitative evidence with qualitative storytelling, brands can connect with audiences intellectually and emotionally.

**Internal alignment and education** are important to ensure accurate messaging. Employees and marketing teams must understand the data, methodology, and implications behind sustainability initiatives. Well-informed internal stakeholders can communicate confidently, answer questions from consumers or media, and act as authentic advocates. This alignment prevents misrepresentation and strengthens the integrity of data-driven messaging.

**Continuous measurement and improvement** are fundamental. Sustainability data is not static; it evolves with operational changes, new technologies, and updated benchmarks. Regular monitoring and reporting allow brands to track progress, identify areas for improvement, and refine messaging over time. Demonstrating continuous improvement signals long-term commitment and enhances credibility with stakeholders.

**Consumer engagement and empowerment** are enhanced through data-backed messaging. Providing clear, actionable information allows consumers to make informed choices and participate in sustainability efforts. For example, sharing a product's carbon footprint or instructions for responsible disposal empowers consumers to align their actions with the brand's purpose, fostering loyalty and advocacy.

**Risk mitigation and accountability** are additional benefits. Data-driven sustainability messaging reduces reputational and regulatory risks by ensuring that claims are verifiable and accurate. Brands that rely on evidence-based communication are better prepared to respond to stakeholder inquiries, audits, or scrutiny from watchdogs, protecting both credibility and market position.

## Inclusive and Responsible Brand Narratives

**Inclusive and Responsible Brand Narratives** are essential for brands seeking to resonate authentically with diverse audiences while upholding ethical, social, and environmental responsibility. In today's conscious consumer landscape, stakeholders expect brands not only to communicate purpose but to do so in a way that reflects inclusivity, equity, and accountability. An inclusive narrative ensures that all stakeholders feel represented and respected, while responsible storytelling aligns messaging with the brand's actions, values, and societal impact. Together, these approaches strengthen credibility, loyalty, and long-term brand equity.

At its core, **inclusive brand narratives** consider diversity across gender, ethnicity, culture, ability, socio-economic background, and geography. Brands must ensure that marketing messages, campaigns, and content do not inadvertently marginalize or stereotype any group.

Inclusion goes beyond token representation; it requires thoughtful, authentic storytelling that reflects the lived experiences of diverse stakeholders. By actively listening to and integrating the perspectives of different communities, brands can create narratives that resonate more deeply and foster emotional connection.

**Responsible narratives** are anchored in authenticity, transparency, and ethical consistency. Brands must ensure that their storytelling aligns with actual practices, policies, and impact initiatives. For instance, a brand promoting gender equality should demonstrate fair labor practices, equitable pay, and leadership opportunities for women across its organization. Responsible narratives avoid exaggeration or selective storytelling that could mislead consumers or be perceived as virtue signaling, thereby preventing reputational risk and building trust.

**Representation matters** in inclusive narratives. Marketing, advertising, and communication materials should depict diverse individuals in meaningful roles, not just as background characters. Product development, campaigns, and customer engagement strategies should reflect the needs and perspectives of various communities. Inclusive narratives ensure that stakeholders see themselves in the brand story, fostering relevance, connection, and loyalty.

**Integration across organizational functions** is crucial. Inclusive and responsible storytelling cannot be confined to marketing or communications; it must be embedded in product design, service delivery, customer support, corporate social responsibility (CSR) initiatives, and internal culture. For example, inclusive product design considers accessibility, while corporate policies reinforce equitable practices. A brand that aligns internal and external narratives demonstrates authenticity, reducing the risk of perceived hypocrisy or greenwashing.

**Engagement and collaboration** strengthen inclusivity. Brands can partner with diverse communities, experts, and organizations to co-create content, initiatives, or products. This approach ensures that messaging reflects authentic voices and experiences, rather than assumptions or stereotypes. Collaborative narratives resonate more effectively because they reflect lived reality and demonstrate respect for the stakeholders represented.

**Transparency and accountability** underpin responsible storytelling. Brands should openly share progress, challenges, and measurable impact in social, environmental, and ethical initiatives. By reporting both successes and areas for improvement, brands demonstrate honesty and foster trust. Data-backed evidence, third-party verification, and clear communication reinforce the integrity of the narrative, making it credible and defensible.

**Avoiding exclusion and harm** is a key principle. Inclusive narratives require brands to evaluate content for potential bias, insensitivity, or unintentional offense. This includes careful review of language, imagery, and messaging frameworks. Brands must proactively prevent exclusionary messaging and respond swiftly to feedback or missteps, reinforcing a commitment to continuous learning and improvement.

**Consumer empowerment** is enhanced by inclusive and responsible narratives. When stakeholders see themselves represented and feel that the brand shares their values, they are more likely to engage, advocate, and form lasting emotional connections. Brands that communicate responsibility alongside inclusion encourage conscious consumer behavior, such as choosing ethical products, participating in sustainability initiatives, or supporting social programs.

**Long-term brand purpose and loyalty** are strengthened through inclusive and responsible storytelling. Brands that consistently reflect diverse perspectives, ethical practices, and societal impact build credibility and differentiate themselves in competitive markets. This alignment between narrative and action enhances stakeholder trust, drives advocacy, and creates resilient brand equity over time.

Finally, **cultural sensitivity and adaptability** are critical. Brands operating in global markets must tailor narratives to local values, norms, and expectations while maintaining core principles of inclusivity and responsibility. Understanding regional context ensures that messaging resonates meaningfully, avoids misinterpretation, and reinforces authenticity across geographies.

## Crisis Communication and Reputation Management

**Crisis Communication and Reputation Management** are critical capabilities for brands operating in today's highly connected, transparent, and conscious consumer environment. In a world where information spreads rapidly through digital channels, a single misstep—whether related to sustainability, ethics, or corporate behavior—can quickly escalate into a reputational crisis. Effective crisis communication and proactive reputation management not only mitigate damage but also reinforce trust, credibility, and long-term brand equity when executed with transparency, accountability, and strategic foresight.

At its core, **crisis communication** involves anticipating, responding to, and managing events that could negatively impact a brand's reputation, stakeholder trust, or operational continuity. Crises may stem from environmental incidents, ethical lapses, product recalls, regulatory violations, social controversies, or public backlash against perceived hypocrisy in sustainability or social responsibility claims. The ability to respond swiftly, transparently, and consistently can significantly influence stakeholder perceptions and the overall resilience of the brand.

**Proactive preparedness** is foundational to effective crisis communication. Brands must establish crisis management frameworks, including clearly defined roles, communication protocols, and escalation procedures. Scenario planning, risk assessments, and media training help ensure that teams are ready to respond effectively under pressure. By anticipating potential vulnerabilities, organizations can reduce response times, manage narratives, and maintain control over messaging rather than reacting reactively in a chaotic environment.

**Transparency and honesty** are essential during a crisis. Stakeholders expect brands to acknowledge issues openly, provide accurate information, and communicate both immediate actions and long-term solutions. Attempts to obscure facts, shift blame, or downplay the situation often exacerbate reputational damage. Transparent communication demonstrates accountability, reinforces trust, and signals that the brand is committed to rectifying problems rather than evading responsibility.

**Consistency across channels** is critical. In today's digital landscape, information travels across social media, news outlets, investor communications, and internal channels almost instantaneously. Inconsistent messaging can create confusion, amplify negative perception, and fuel speculation. Coordinated communication ensures that all stakeholders receive the same accurate information, reinforcing credibility and trust during turbulent times.

**Empathy and stakeholder-centric messaging** play a vital role. Crisis communication must address the concerns of affected parties, demonstrate understanding of their perspectives, and outline actionable steps to mitigate harm. Whether the audience includes consumers, employees, communities, or regulators, empathetic communication fosters goodwill, reduces hostility, and positions the brand as responsible and conscientious.

**Reputation management** extends beyond immediate crisis response to encompass long-term strategies for maintaining and enhancing brand equity. A strong reputation is built on consistent delivery of promises, ethical behavior, and effective stakeholder engagement. By cultivating trust and demonstrating reliability over time, brands increase resilience, making them less vulnerable to reputational shocks when crises arise.

**Monitoring and rapid response systems** are integral to reputation management. Continuous tracking of media coverage, social sentiment, and stakeholder feedback allows brands to identify emerging issues before they escalate. Early detection facilitates prompt engagement, strategic messaging, and corrective action, reducing the risk of widespread reputational harm.

**Corrective and preventive measures** reinforce credibility post-crisis. Brands must not only resolve the immediate issue but also implement structural or operational changes to prevent recurrence. Sharing these improvements publicly demonstrates accountability, reinforces trust, and transforms a crisis into an opportunity to showcase organizational learning and commitment to continuous improvement.

**Internal alignment and employee communication** are equally important. Employees are often brand ambassadors, and their understanding of the crisis, messaging protocols, and actions to take ensures consistent communication externally. Empowered and informed employees can help maintain credibility and reduce misinformation during challenging situations.

**Long-term brand narrative** plays a role in mitigating reputational risk. Brands that consistently communicate purpose, authenticity, sustainability, and ethical practices develop stakeholder loyalty that can buffer against negative events. A strong, purpose-driven reputation provides context and perspective, helping audiences view crises in light of the brand's broader values and commitment.

Finally, **recovery and rebuilding trust** are ongoing processes. After the immediate crisis has been addressed, brands must engage in sustained communication, demonstrate impact of corrective measures, and reaffirm commitments to purpose and stakeholder responsibility. Authenticity, transparency, and continued evidence of ethical practices are essential to restoring confidence and reinforcing long-term credibility.

# Digital and Data-Driven Sustainable Marketing

# Sustainable Digital Practices and Carbon Footprint

**Sustainable Digital Practices and Carbon Footprint** are increasingly important considerations for brands and organizations in the 21st century, as digital operations, marketing, and consumer engagement continue to expand. While digital technologies offer efficiency, scalability, and reach, they also carry environmental impacts—primarily through energy consumption, data storage, cloud services, and digital device production. Integrating sustainable digital practices helps organizations reduce their carbon footprint, demonstrate environmental responsibility, and align with conscious consumer expectations.

At its core, **sustainable digital practices** involve designing, deploying, and managing digital infrastructure and operations in a way that minimizes environmental impact while maintaining performance and user experience. This includes optimizing data centers, selecting energy-efficient cloud services, reducing redundant digital processes, and implementing responsible IT lifecycle management. By evaluating the environmental consequences of digital operations, organizations can make strategic decisions that reduce energy use, carbon emissions, and electronic waste.

**Carbon footprint in digital operations** refers to the total greenhouse gas emissions associated with producing, using, and maintaining digital technologies. This includes electricity used by servers, networks, and devices; emissions from manufacturing and disposal of hardware; and indirect impacts such as emissions associated with cloud service providers. As digital adoption grows, the carbon footprint of IT operations can become a significant component of an organization's overall environmental impact, making measurement and mitigation critical.

**Energy efficiency** is a cornerstone of sustainable digital practices. Organizations can adopt low-energy servers, virtualized infrastructure, and optimized cloud solutions to reduce energy consumption. Data center efficiency measures—such as Power

Usage Effectiveness (PUE), renewable energy sourcing, and advanced cooling systems—also help lower the carbon footprint while maintaining high availability and performance. Optimizing digital processes, reducing redundant storage, and minimizing unnecessary data transfer further contribute to energy savings.

**Sustainable content and digital marketing** are essential elements. Large-scale digital campaigns, video streaming, and heavy web content consume significant energy and bandwidth. Organizations can reduce impact by optimizing website design for efficiency, using compressed media formats, limiting auto-play videos, and promoting responsible digital behavior among users. Sustainable digital marketing not only reduces environmental footprint but also enhances brand reputation by demonstrating awareness of digital sustainability challenges.

**Lifecycle management of digital devices** plays a role in sustainability. This includes selecting energy-efficient devices, extending device lifespan through repair or refurbishment, and responsible recycling or disposal at end-of-life. Minimizing e-waste reduces environmental contamination and resource depletion while promoting a circular approach to technology. Brands that implement responsible device management can communicate tangible sustainability outcomes to consumers and stakeholders.

**Measurement and reporting** are critical for credible sustainability practices. Brands should quantify digital carbon footprints, track energy consumption, and report reductions transparently. Tools and frameworks such as the Greenhouse Gas Protocol, ISO 14064, or cloud provider sustainability reports allow organizations to monitor and benchmark impact. Data-backed reporting strengthens credibility, ensures transparency, and aligns digital operations with broader organizational sustainability goals.

**Consumer engagement and awareness** can also be enhanced through sustainable digital practices. Brands can educate users about reducing energy consumption while using digital services, such as limiting high-definition streaming or optimizing cloud storage. Encouraging conscious digital behavior strengthens the brand's purpose-driven narrative and positions it as a thought leader in responsible digital consumption.

**Innovation and technology adoption** support sustainability. Cloud migration to providers using renewable energy, AI-based optimization of server workloads, and edge computing to reduce data transfer are examples of technological solutions that reduce environmental impact. Continuous innovation ensures that digital operations remain efficient, scalable, and aligned with evolving sustainability benchmarks.

**Regulatory compliance and stakeholder expectations** increasingly drive sustainable digital practices. Governments, investors, and consumers are paying attention to the carbon impact of digital operations. Proactively adopting green IT policies, carbon reduction initiatives, and sustainable digital strategies positions brands as responsible leaders and reduces regulatory and reputational risks.

Finally, sustainable digital practices are integral to **long-term brand purpose and credibility**. Brands that demonstrate accountability in their digital footprint reinforce trust, differentiate themselves in competitive markets, and show alignment with conscious consumer values. By integrating sustainability into digital strategy, organizations not only reduce environmental impact but also strengthen operational efficiency, stakeholder engagement, and long-term resilience.

## Responsible Use of Data and Consumer Privacy

**Responsible Use of Data and Consumer Privacy** is a critical dimension of sustainable and ethical marketing in today's digital economy. With data becoming a core asset for brands—driving personalization, targeted marketing, predictive analytics, and customer engagement—the responsibility to handle consumer information with care has never been more important. Conscious consumers, regulators, and investors expect brands to respect privacy, maintain transparency, and use data in ways that uphold ethical standards, protect trust, and reduce reputational risk.

At its core, responsible data use involves **collecting, storing, and analyzing consumer information in ways that are lawful, transparent, and aligned with both ethical standards and brand values**. This includes ensuring informed consent, clearly communicating how data will be used, and limiting collection to what is necessary for service delivery or value creation. By respecting these principles, brands build trust, foster long-term engagement, and demonstrate that they prioritize stakeholder welfare over purely commercial objectives.

**Consumer privacy** is central to responsible data practices. Organizations must safeguard personal information against unauthorized access, breaches, or misuse. This includes implementing strong cybersecurity measures, encryption, secure storage solutions, and regular audits. Privacy policies should be clear, accessible, and written in a way that consumers can easily understand. Transparent communication about how data is used, shared, and protected reinforces accountability and empowers consumers to make informed decisions about their personal information.

**Ethical data practices** go beyond compliance with regulations such as the General Data Protection Regulation (GDPR), California Consumer Privacy Act (CCPA), or other regional data privacy laws. Ethical practices include avoiding manipulative or intrusive data use, preventing discriminatory algorithms, and ensuring that analytics and AI applications do not harm individuals or communities. Brands that demonstrate ethical stewardship of data strengthen credibility, differentiate themselves, and create long-term value beyond legal compliance.

**Transparency in data use** is essential. Brands should clearly communicate the purpose of data collection, how it will be processed, and with whom it may be shared. Providing consumers with options to control their data—such as opting out of tracking, managing preferences, or deleting personal information—demonstrates respect for autonomy and fosters trust. Transparency also mitigates reputational risks by reducing the likelihood of consumer backlash or accusations of misuse.

**Data minimization and purpose limitation** are key strategies for responsible use. Brands should collect only the data necessary to deliver services, improve experiences, or support sustainability initiatives. Limiting the scope of data reduces exposure to security risks, simplifies compliance, and signals to consumers that the organization values privacy over unnecessary commercial gain. Purpose limitation ensures that collected data is not repurposed for unrelated or potentially exploitative activities.

**Consumer empowerment and engagement** are enhanced when brands adopt responsible data practices. By giving consumers control over their personal information and educating them about how their data contributes to improved services or sustainability efforts, brands can create stronger relationships and foster loyalty. For example, data used to optimize energy consumption in smart products or to enhance recycling programs can be presented as a value-driven initiative that benefits both the consumer and the planet.

**Cross-functional integration** is critical. IT, legal, marketing, and operational teams must collaborate to ensure data practices are consistent, ethical, and secure. Governance frameworks, regular audits, and staff training are essential for maintaining high standards of privacy and responsible use. By embedding data ethics into organizational culture, brands demonstrate commitment and accountability at all levels.

**Risk mitigation** is another important dimension. Mishandling data can result in regulatory penalties, reputational damage, and loss of consumer trust. Proactively implementing privacy safeguards, ethical guidelines, and transparent reporting reduces these risks and ensures resilience. Brands that prioritize responsible data use also position themselves as trustworthy partners in increasingly privacy-conscious markets.

Finally, responsible data practices reinforce **long-term brand purpose and credibility**. In an era where trust is a key differentiator, brands that handle consumer data responsibly demonstrate integrity, transparency, and alignment with stakeholder expectations. This not only protects reputation but also strengthens loyalty, advocacy, and sustainable growth.

## AI, Automation, and Ethical Marketing

**AI, Automation, and Ethical Marketing** represent a transformative intersection of technology, efficiency, and responsibility in modern marketing strategies. Artificial Intelligence (AI) and automation have revolutionized how brands understand consumer behavior, segment audiences, optimize campaigns, and deliver personalized experiences. However, with great technological power comes great responsibility: brands must ensure that these tools are used ethically, respecting consumer rights, avoiding bias, and maintaining transparency while still leveraging the efficiency and insights that AI and automation provide.

At its core, **AI in marketing** involves using machine learning, predictive analytics, natural language processing, and other computational techniques to analyze large datasets, identify patterns, and make informed decisions. This enables hyper-personalization, optimized targeting, content recommendations, dynamic pricing, and predictive customer engagement. Automation streamlines repetitive tasks such as email campaigns, social media posting, and chat-based customer service, freeing human resources to focus on strategic, creative, and relational aspects of marketing. Together, AI and automation enhance operational efficiency, improve ROI, and allow brands to deliver more relevant, timely, and engaging experiences.

**Ethical marketing** ensures that AI-driven and automated processes operate in ways that are fair, responsible, and transparent. This begins with **data ethics**: ensuring that AI algorithms use consumer data with informed consent, protect privacy, and avoid manipulative tactics. Responsible brands implement robust data governance frameworks, anonymize sensitive information, and clearly communicate how data is used in AI-driven personalization and decision-making. This transparency fosters trust and reinforces the brand's commitment to consumer rights.

**Bias and fairness** are key ethical considerations. AI systems can unintentionally perpetuate discrimination or favoritism if trained on incomplete or biased datasets. For example, predictive algorithms might favor certain demographics over others in ad targeting or product recommendations. Ethical marketing requires rigorous monitoring, testing, and correction of AI models to ensure fairness, inclusivity, and equitable treatment of all consumer segments. By proactively addressing bias, brands demonstrate social responsibility while safeguarding reputation and credibility.

**Transparency and explainability** are critical. Consumers and stakeholders increasingly demand clarity about how AI-driven decisions affect them. Brands that provide understandable explanations for recommendations, personalized offers, or automated interactions create trust and reduce skepticism. Ethical marketing ensures that automation does not obscure decision-making processes, mislead consumers, or manipulate behavior without informed consent.

**Automation ethics** extends to human oversight. While automation increases efficiency, brands must maintain human involvement in critical decisions, especially those affecting sensitive customer interactions or ethical judgment. For instance, automated customer service should have escalation paths to human representatives, and AI-driven marketing strategies should be regularly reviewed to ensure alignment with brand values and ethical standards. This balance prevents overreliance on machines and safeguards accountability.

**Consumer empowerment** is another pillar of ethical AI marketing. Brands should provide options for consumers to control personalization, opt out of AI-driven targeting, and understand how their data contributes to automated decision-making. Empowered consumers are more likely to trust and engage with the brand, reinforcing loyalty and long-term relationship building.

**Sustainability integration** is a growing focus in AI and automation. Brands can use AI to optimize resource allocation, reduce energy consumption, minimize waste in supply chains, and design sustainable products or campaigns. By aligning AI capabilities with environmental and social goals, companies demonstrate that technology can be leveraged responsibly to achieve both operational and ethical objectives.

**Regulatory compliance** is another essential dimension. Emerging laws and industry standards around AI, automation, and data use—such as GDPR, CCPA, and AI ethics guidelines—require brands to ensure that marketing practices meet legal and societal expectations. Compliance not only mitigates risk but signals to consumers and stakeholders that the brand is accountable, responsible, and forward-thinking.

**Innovation with accountability** ensures that brands maintain competitive advantage without compromising values. By embracing AI and automation while adhering to ethical principles, organizations can deliver highly effective, efficient, and sustainable marketing campaigns. Ethical implementation becomes a differentiator in a market where conscious consumers value integrity, transparency, and social responsibility alongside performance.

Finally, **long-term brand trust and loyalty** are reinforced when AI and automation are used ethically. Brands that prioritize fairness, transparency, and responsible data use create emotional and rational trust with consumers. Ethical AI marketing strengthens credibility, mitigates reputational risk, and ensures that technology serves human and societal interests rather than exploiting them.

## Performance Marketing with Purpose

**Performance Marketing with Purpose** represents a strategic evolution in marketing where brands focus not only on measurable outcomes—such as clicks, conversions, and ROI—but also on aligning campaigns with their broader purpose, values, and sustainability goals. In a conscious consumer landscape, transactional success alone is no longer sufficient; brands are expected to create meaningful, responsible engagement while driving measurable business results. Combining performance marketing with purpose allows organizations to achieve both financial and societal impact, strengthening brand equity and fostering loyalty.

At its core, **performance marketing** is data-driven and outcome-oriented. It leverages digital channels such as search engines, social media, email, and programmatic advertising to deliver targeted campaigns that can be measured and optimized in real time. Metrics such as cost-per-click, conversion rates, lifetime value, and return on ad spend are central to evaluating campaign success. When infused with purpose, these campaigns not only optimize metrics but also communicate values, highlight sustainability initiatives, or support social impact causes that resonate with conscious consumers.

**Integrating purpose into performance marketing** begins with clearly defining the brand's mission and ethical commitments. Purpose-driven campaigns convey more than just product benefits; they demonstrate how the brand contributes positively to society, the environment, or ethical practices. For example, a campaign promoting a recycled product can highlight the environmental benefits of responsible consumption, creating emotional resonance while driving measurable conversions. Purpose serves as a guiding principle for creative messaging, targeting, and channel selection.

**Consumer engagement is enhanced** when performance marketing incorporates purpose. Conscious consumers are more likely to interact with campaigns that reflect their values and demonstrate authentic impact. Metrics such as click-through rates, engagement rates, and sharing behavior are often higher when campaigns communicate social or environmental benefits alongside product offerings. Purpose-driven messaging also strengthens brand recall and emotional connection, creating loyalty that extends beyond the immediate transaction.

**Transparency and authenticity** are key to success. Purpose-driven performance marketing must be grounded in real actions and verifiable impact. Claims about sustainability, social initiatives, or ethical practices must be supported by data, certifications, or credible stories. Failure to substantiate purpose-oriented messaging risks consumer skepticism, backlash, and reputational damage, undermining both performance metrics and long-term trust.

**Targeting and personalization** can be aligned with purpose. AI and analytics tools allow brands to segment audiences based on interests, behaviors, or values, ensuring that purpose-driven messaging reaches individuals who are most likely to engage and advocate. For instance, campaigns highlighting eco-friendly products can target consumers interested in sustainability, maximizing both relevance and ROI. Purpose alignment enhances engagement quality, not just quantity.

**Measurement frameworks** for performance marketing with purpose go beyond traditional KPIs. While standard metrics like conversions and revenue remain important, brands also track indicators of impact and engagement related to purpose. These may include social shares of sustainability content, participation in cause-driven initiatives, or behavior change among consumers (e.g., adopting eco-friendly practices). By integrating these metrics, organizations can evaluate both business and societal outcomes.

**Innovation in creative execution** strengthens purpose-driven performance campaigns. Storytelling, interactive content, gamification, and experiential marketing can convey brand purpose while driving measurable actions. For example, an interactive online campaign encouraging users to reduce carbon footprints or participate in charitable programs can generate engagement, data insights, and actionable outcomes simultaneously. Innovation ensures that purpose and performance reinforce each other effectively.

**Cross-functional alignment** is critical. Marketing teams, sustainability officers, product developers, and analytics experts must collaborate to ensure that campaigns reflect authentic purpose, deliver measurable results, and comply with ethical standards. Internal alignment prevents miscommunication, enhances credibility, and ensures that performance marketing supports the broader strategic vision of the brand.

**Risk mitigation and accountability** are also essential. Purpose-driven campaigns must be carefully monitored to avoid overpromising or misleading claims, which can undermine both trust and performance metrics. Ongoing evaluation, transparency, and responsiveness to consumer feedback ensure that campaigns remain credible, effective, and aligned with brand values.

Finally, **long-term brand equity and loyalty** are reinforced when performance marketing aligns with purpose. Campaigns that demonstrate measurable impact while reflecting core values foster deeper emotional connection, advocacy, and repeat engagement. Purpose-driven performance marketing transforms transactional interactions into meaningful experiences, building sustainable brand-consumer relationships that extend beyond individual campaigns.

## Measuring Digital Impact Responsibly

**Measuring Digital Impact Responsibly** is an essential practice for modern brands aiming to balance performance, accountability, and sustainability in an increasingly digital and conscious marketplace. As organizations leverage digital platforms, marketing technologies, and online engagement strategies, they generate vast amounts of data and influence consumer behavior. Measuring the impact of these activities responsibly ensures that brands can evaluate performance accurately, maintain ethical standards, minimize unintended negative consequences, and align digital strategies with both business goals and broader societal values.

At its core, responsible measurement involves **tracking digital metrics in a way that is transparent, ethical, and contextualized**. Traditional digital KPIs—such as clicks, impressions, conversion rates, and engagement—remain important, but responsible measurement goes further by considering the environmental, social, and ethical dimensions of digital activity. For example, campaigns that rely heavily on energy-intensive streaming, cloud storage, or repeated automated communications contribute to carbon emissions, electronic waste, and information overload. Brands that incorporate these considerations into their measurement framework demonstrate accountability beyond mere performance metrics.

**Transparency in measurement** is fundamental. Brands should clearly define what is being measured, how data is collected, and how insights will be used. Transparent reporting ensures stakeholders—including consumers, employees, and investors—understand the scope, limitations, and implications of digital impact assessments. For instance, sharing data on both engagement and environmental footprint allows audiences to see the trade-offs and responsible decision-making involved in digital strategies.

**Incorporating ethical considerations** is a central aspect of responsible measurement. Brands must ensure that data collection, analysis, and reporting respect consumer privacy, comply with regulations such as GDPR and CCPA, and avoid manipulative practices. Metrics should not incentivize harmful behavior, exploit vulnerable populations, or reinforce bias. Responsible measurement evaluates digital success in a way that aligns with ethical marketing and corporate values, fostering trust and credibility.

**Environmental impact assessment** is increasingly critical in digital operations. Measuring energy consumption from server usage, cloud computing, streaming, or online ad delivery allows brands to understand the carbon footprint of their digital campaigns. By quantifying environmental impact and setting reduction targets, organizations can make informed decisions about platform selection, campaign design, and operational efficiency, integrating sustainability directly into digital performance measurement.

**Social impact measurement** is equally important. Digital campaigns influence community behavior, awareness, and social outcomes. Measuring responsible engagement includes assessing the quality of interactions, community sentiment, knowledge dissemination, and behavioral changes prompted by digital initiatives. For instance, a campaign promoting sustainable consumer choices can be evaluated not only by click-through rates but by its actual influence on purchasing behavior, participation in eco-friendly practices, or advocacy.

**Holistic metrics** combine traditional performance indicators with environmental and social considerations. By integrating financial, operational, ethical, and sustainability metrics into a unified framework, brands can obtain a comprehensive view of digital impact. This approach allows organizations to identify trade-offs, optimize strategies, and demonstrate accountability across multiple dimensions of performance.

**Third-party validation and standards** enhance credibility. Leveraging independent audits, industry benchmarks, and recognized frameworks—such as ISO standards for digital sustainability, carbon reporting protocols, or digital ethics guidelines—ensures that measurement practices are rigorous, comparable, and trustworthy. External validation strengthens stakeholder confidence in reported outcomes and mitigates reputational risks associated with unverified claims.

**Continuous improvement and learning** are vital components. Digital technologies and platforms evolve rapidly, and responsible measurement must adapt to emerging tools, channels, and consumer behaviors. Regular evaluation of metrics, methodologies, and assumptions allows brands to refine campaigns, enhance accuracy, and reduce negative consequences over time. Learning from past initiatives also strengthens strategic planning and innovation in digital sustainability.

**Stakeholder engagement** amplifies responsible measurement. Engaging consumers, employees, investors, and community members in the evaluation process provides context, feedback, and validation. Co-created metrics, participatory reporting, and transparent communication foster trust, empower audiences, and ensure that measurement reflects shared values and societal expectations.

Finally, responsible digital impact measurement reinforces **long-term brand credibility, trust, and purpose alignment**. Brands that track and report their digital footprint ethically, transparently, and holistically differentiate themselves in conscious consumer markets. By integrating performance, environmental stewardship, social responsibility, and ethical oversight into measurement frameworks, organizations can optimize digital strategies while maintaining accountability, authenticity, and stakeholder confidence.

# Influencer, Community, and Partnership Strategies

# Values-Based Influencer Selection

**Values-Based Influencer Selection** is a strategic approach in modern marketing that emphasizes aligning influencer partnerships with a brand's core values, mission, and purpose. In an era of conscious consumerism, audiences increasingly scrutinize not only what brands promote but also who represents them. Selecting influencers based on shared ethical principles, social responsibility, and sustainability commitments ensures authenticity, strengthens credibility, and amplifies purpose-driven messaging while reducing reputational risks associated with misalignment or superficial endorsements.

At its core, values-based influencer selection goes beyond superficial metrics such as follower count, engagement rate, or reach. While traditional influencer marketing prioritizes audience size and immediate ROI, a values-driven approach evaluates alignment with the brand's purpose, ethical standards, and social or environmental commitments. For instance, a sustainable fashion brand would prioritize influencers who demonstrate genuine interest in eco-conscious living, ethical sourcing, or minimalism rather than those promoting mass consumption. This alignment ensures that messaging feels authentic and resonates with conscious audiences.

**Authenticity and credibility** are central to this approach. Influencers who genuinely embody the values of the brand can communicate messages more persuasively and foster trust among their followers. Audiences are quick to detect incongruence between an influencer's behavior and the brand they represent. Misalignment can lead to skepticism, backlash, and reduced campaign effectiveness. By carefully selecting influencers whose lifestyles, beliefs, and public engagement reflect the brand's principles, organizations strengthen both campaign impact and long-term reputation.

**Ethical considerations** play a critical role. Brands must ensure that influencers do not engage in behavior, partnerships, or messaging that contradicts ethical marketing principles, sustainability goals, or societal norms. Vetting processes include reviewing past content, social responsibility involvement, and public perception. This diligence helps prevent inadvertent associations with controversy, unethical practices, or greenwashing, protecting the brand's integrity and consumer trust.

**Audience alignment** is also essential. Beyond personal values, influencers should have audiences that share the brand's target demographics and psychographics, particularly with respect to conscious consumption and purpose-driven behavior. By engaging followers who are predisposed to value sustainability, social responsibility, or ethical practices, brands enhance relevance, engagement, and conversion potential while reinforcing their purpose-driven positioning.

**Long-term partnerships** are preferable to one-off collaborations. Consistent engagement with influencers who embody brand values allows narratives to develop organically, fostering deeper emotional connection and advocacy. Long-term partnerships also signal genuine commitment rather than transactional marketing, enhancing credibility and brand authenticity in the eyes of conscious consumers.

**Measurement and accountability** remain important even in values-based selection. Brands should track both traditional performance metrics—such as engagement, reach, and conversions—and impact indicators related to values alignment, such as audience perception, sentiment analysis, and behavioral change. These insights ensure that influencer partnerships deliver both business results and purpose-driven outcomes.

**Transparency in collaboration** strengthens trust. Brands should clearly communicate the nature of partnerships, sponsorships, or campaigns to audiences. Authentic disclosure builds credibility for both the influencer and the brand, reinforcing the notion that the campaign is aligned with shared values rather than purely commercial objectives.

**Diversity and inclusion** are key components. Values-based influencer selection considers representation across gender, ethnicity, culture, and socio-economic backgrounds to reflect both brand values and audience diversity. Inclusive partnerships ensure messaging resonates broadly, promotes equity, and avoids reinforcing stereotypes or exclusionary practices.

**Integration with broader strategy** is critical. Influencer campaigns should complement overall brand purpose, sustainability initiatives, and ethical marketing efforts. By aligning influencer storytelling with corporate messaging, social campaigns, and digital content strategies, brands create a coherent narrative that reinforces authenticity, strengthens engagement, and amplifies societal impact.

Finally, values-based influencer selection contributes to **long-term brand trust and loyalty**. Partnerships that authentically reflect brand values enhance credibility, foster advocacy, and create emotional resonance with audiences. By carefully vetting, selecting, and nurturing influencers who genuinely embody shared principles, organizations strengthen both performance and purpose, ensuring that marketing efforts resonate meaningfully in a conscious consumer world.

## Community-Led Brand Advocacy

**Community-Led Brand Advocacy** is a marketing and engagement strategy that leverages the authentic voices, experiences, and networks of a brand's community to build credibility, trust, and sustainable influence. Unlike traditional top-down marketing campaigns where the brand directly controls messaging, community-led advocacy empowers customers, employees, and other stakeholders to share experiences, insights, and endorsements organically. This approach resonates particularly strongly in a conscious consumer world, where authenticity, shared values, and peer validation are increasingly critical to purchasing decisions.

At its core, community-led advocacy focuses on **engaging stakeholders as active participants** rather than passive recipients of messaging. Brands cultivate relationships with their audience by providing value, creating meaningful experiences, and fostering shared purpose. When members of the community genuinely connect with the brand's mission—whether it is sustainability, social impact, or ethical business practices—they naturally become advocates, sharing their enthusiasm and influencing peers. This grassroots promotion is often more persuasive and credible than traditional advertising because it originates from trusted voices rather than the brand itself.

**Authenticity and trust** are central to community-led advocacy. Advocates are motivated by genuine belief in the brand's values and practices, rather than by financial incentives alone. Brands must ensure that their products, services, and initiatives consistently reflect stated values, as any disconnect can quickly undermine credibility. By demonstrating transparency, ethical conduct, and alignment with stakeholder expectations, organizations foster advocacy that is enduring and credible.

**Empowerment and engagement** are key drivers. Brands must actively engage their community by providing platforms for discussion, sharing, and collaboration. This can include social media groups, forums, ambassador programs, co-creation projects, or interactive campaigns. Empowering individuals to contribute ideas, share experiences, or participate in sustainability initiatives not only strengthens their emotional connection to the brand but also amplifies the reach and impact of advocacy organically.

**Shared values and purpose** form the foundation of community-led advocacy. Successful programs align the interests of the brand with those of its stakeholders. For instance, a brand committed to environmental sustainability can encourage community members to participate in recycling initiatives, conservation projects, or awareness campaigns. By aligning advocacy opportunities with values that matter to the community, brands create genuine engagement and deepen loyalty.

**Measurement and feedback loops** are essential to ensure that community-led advocacy is effective and aligned with broader objectives. Traditional marketing metrics such as reach, engagement, and conversion remain relevant, but qualitative indicators—such as sentiment analysis, peer-to-peer recommendations, and participation in initiatives—provide insight into the depth and authenticity of advocacy. Regular feedback from community members allows brands to refine programs, address concerns, and co-create initiatives that resonate meaningfully.

**Diversity and inclusivity** strengthen community-led advocacy. By involving stakeholders from various demographics, geographies, and backgrounds, brands ensure that advocacy reflects a wide spectrum of experiences and perspectives. Inclusive communities foster broader engagement, encourage innovative ideas, and strengthen the perception that the brand represents and values all stakeholders.

**Integration with brand strategy** ensures that community-led advocacy reinforces purpose and long-term goals. Advocacy initiatives should align with corporate mission, sustainability objectives, and ethical standards. This coherence ensures that community-generated messaging is consistent with the brand's overarching narrative and reinforces credibility, avoiding confusion or misrepresentation.

**Digital platforms and social networks** amplify community-led advocacy. Social media, online communities, and interactive apps enable advocates to share content, experiences, and endorsements widely. By facilitating peer-to-peer sharing and engagement, brands can expand reach organically while maintaining authenticity, as audiences tend to trust messages from real users more than traditional advertisements.

**Recognition and relationship-building** sustain advocacy. While intrinsic motivation drives authentic advocacy, acknowledging contributions through recognition, access to exclusive content, or participation in co-creation initiatives reinforces engagement. Brands that nurture relationships and show appreciation for their community members foster loyalty and continuous advocacy over time.

Finally, **long-term brand equity** benefits from community-led advocacy. Brands that cultivate authentic, purpose-driven communities experience increased trust, stronger emotional connections, and greater resilience in competitive or crisis situations. Community advocates act as both ambassadors and collaborators, amplifying brand impact while reinforcing ethical and value-driven positioning.

## NGO, Startup, and Government Collaborations

**NGO, Startup, and Government Collaborations** represent a powerful framework for brands seeking to scale their impact, advance sustainability goals, and enhance credibility in a conscious consumer landscape. By partnering with non-governmental organizations (NGOs), innovative startups, and government bodies, brands can leverage complementary expertise, resources, and networks to address social, environmental, and economic challenges more effectively than they could alone. Such collaborations not only drive tangible outcomes but also strengthen purpose-driven narratives, build trust, and demonstrate authentic commitment to societal good.

At its core, **NGO collaborations** provide brands with specialized knowledge, credibility, and community access. NGOs often possess deep expertise in environmental conservation, social welfare, human rights, or education, along with established networks in local communities. By partnering with NGOs, brands can design programs that are informed, contextually relevant, and impactful. For example, a company aiming to reduce plastic waste might collaborate with an environmental NGO to implement recycling initiatives, run awareness campaigns, or develop educational programs. Such partnerships ensure that sustainability initiatives are grounded in expertise and tangible community outcomes.

**Startup collaborations** bring innovation, agility, and cutting-edge solutions to sustainability and purpose-driven initiatives. Startups often specialize in emerging technologies, digital solutions, eco-friendly materials, or circular economy models. Partnering with startups allows established brands to access rapid experimentation, novel approaches, and scalable solutions that may otherwise be unavailable internally. For instance, a fashion brand could collaborate with a startup developing biodegradable fabrics or AI-driven supply chain optimization, accelerating sustainable practices while staying ahead in competitive markets. Startups contribute not only technical expertise but also creative thinking that challenges traditional processes and encourages continuous improvement.

**Government collaborations** provide regulatory support, legitimacy, and broader societal impact. Governments play a critical role in setting standards, providing incentives, and implementing large-scale initiatives that require multi-stakeholder participation. Brands that engage with government programs—such as renewable energy adoption, waste reduction policies, or social welfare projects—benefit from alignment with public policy, access to funding or grants, and enhanced societal visibility. Additionally, collaboration with government agencies can facilitate scaling initiatives to regional or national levels, increasing reach and impact beyond what a brand could achieve independently.

**Synergistic benefits** emerge from the combination of NGOs, startups, and government partnerships. NGOs bring credibility and on-the-ground expertise, startups provide innovation and agility, and governments offer regulatory alignment and scale. Together, these stakeholders enable brands to design initiatives that are practical, technologically advanced, and widely supported. This integrated approach enhances the effectiveness of sustainability projects, social programs, and purpose-driven campaigns, making the impact measurable and enduring.

**Shared purpose and alignment** are crucial to successful collaborations. All partners must share clearly defined goals, values, and expectations to ensure coherence in execution and messaging. Misaligned objectives can lead to inefficiencies, reputational risk, or diluted impact. Transparent agreements, joint planning, and continuous communication help ensure that partnerships remain focused, accountable, and mutually beneficial.

**Transparency, reporting, and accountability** are essential in multi-stakeholder collaborations. Brands should clearly communicate the roles, contributions, and outcomes of NGO, startup, and government partnerships. Metrics such as environmental impact, social benefits, technology adoption rates, and community engagement help quantify success. Regular reporting fosters stakeholder confidence, demonstrates authenticity, and strengthens the credibility of the initiatives, particularly when external validation or third-party audits are included.

**Community engagement and empowerment** are amplified through these collaborations. NGOs often act as bridges to local communities, startups introduce innovative tools for participation, and governments facilitate large-scale outreach programs. By leveraging these collective resources, brands can design programs that actively involve stakeholders, promote behavioral change, and foster long-term adoption of sustainable or socially responsible practices.

**Risk mitigation** is another important advantage. Collaborative initiatives distribute responsibility across multiple stakeholders, reducing operational, reputational, and regulatory risks for brands. Additionally, diverse expertise helps anticipate challenges, address potential conflicts, and ensure that initiatives comply with legal, social, and environmental standards.

**Innovation, scalability, and impact** are strengthened through these partnerships. Startups provide new technologies or business models, NGOs ensure initiatives are socially and environmentally effective, and governments facilitate scaling through policy support and funding mechanisms. Together, they enable brands to achieve measurable outcomes that are both meaningful and sustainable, reinforcing credibility and stakeholder trust.

Finally, **long-term brand equity and purpose alignment** are enhanced by NGO, startup, and government collaborations. Purpose-driven partnerships demonstrate commitment beyond profit, showcase authenticity, and position the brand as a proactive contributor to societal and environmental progress. Consumers, investors, and communities increasingly value brands that participate in multi-stakeholder solutions, recognizing these efforts as markers of ethical leadership and strategic foresight.

# Co-Creation with Conscious Consumers

**Co-Creation with Conscious Consumers** is a marketing and product development approach that actively involves ethically-minded and sustainability-conscious consumers in shaping products, services, campaigns, and brand initiatives. Unlike traditional top-down strategies, co-creation emphasizes collaboration, dialogue, and shared purpose, enabling brands to align offerings with consumer values, foster loyalty, and drive meaningful impact. In today's conscious consumer world, co-creation strengthens authenticity, enhances relevance, and ensures that brand actions resonate with stakeholders who increasingly seek alignment between their values and the companies they support.

At its core, **co-creation** is about engaging consumers as partners rather than passive recipients. Brands invite conscious consumers to contribute insights, ideas, and feedback on products, services, sustainability initiatives, or marketing campaigns. For example, a brand producing eco-friendly packaging might involve customers in evaluating design options, suggesting materials, or identifying features that minimize environmental impact. This collaborative process empowers consumers, makes them feel valued, and fosters emotional investment in the brand's mission and offerings.

**Consumer trust and authenticity** are central to successful co-creation. Conscious consumers are adept at detecting superficial or performative initiatives. Brands that genuinely involve stakeholders in shaping products or sustainability initiatives demonstrate transparency and integrity. When co-creation is authentic, participants perceive that their input is valued and impactful, creating a sense of shared ownership and reinforcing trust in the brand's purpose-driven agenda.

**Diverse perspectives and inclusivity** strengthen co-creation outcomes. By involving consumers from different demographics, geographies, cultures, and lifestyles, brands ensure that innovations are relevant, accessible, and equitable. Inclusion also helps identify potential blind spots, ethical concerns, or unintended consequences early in the design or campaign process. This inclusive approach aligns with both social responsibility and market relevance, enhancing the credibility and effectiveness of brand initiatives.

**Innovation and relevance** are enhanced through consumer collaboration. Conscious consumers bring first-hand insights into market trends, sustainability preferences, and social priorities. This knowledge allows brands to develop solutions that are not only functional but also ethically and environmentally responsible. Co-created products, services, or campaigns are more likely to resonate with the target audience, drive adoption, and encourage advocacy.

**Transparency and feedback loops** are critical to sustaining co-creation. Brands must clearly communicate how consumer input is collected, evaluated, and implemented. Providing updates on progress, acknowledging contributions, and demonstrating the tangible impact of consumer ideas reinforces engagement and trust. These feedback mechanisms ensure that co-creation is meaningful rather than tokenistic, maintaining credibility in conscious consumer communities.

**Behavioral influence and advocacy** are natural byproducts of co-creation. Consumers who participate in shaping brand initiatives are more likely to promote, defend, and advocate for the brand within their networks. This organic advocacy amplifies reach, builds credibility, and strengthens the emotional connection between the brand and its community. When conscious consumers share the brand's purpose-driven narrative authentically, it enhances both engagement and impact.

**Integration with sustainability and purpose** is essential. Co-creation initiatives should align with the brand's broader mission, ethical standards, and environmental or social goals. For instance, collaborative campaigns focused on reducing carbon footprints, ethical sourcing, or community welfare reinforce both consumer values and the brand's purpose. This alignment ensures that co-creation is not just a marketing tactic but a strategic component of the brand's long-term mission.

**Digital platforms and technology** enable scalable co-creation. Online communities, social media, interactive surveys, mobile apps, and virtual workshops allow brands to engage large and diverse groups of conscious consumers efficiently. Digital tools facilitate real-time collaboration, idea sharing, and voting, creating an inclusive and participatory experience while capturing valuable insights for decision-making.

**Measurement and impact assessment** are important to validate co-creation efforts. Brands should track both qualitative and quantitative outcomes, including consumer engagement, sentiment, adoption of co-created solutions, and alignment with sustainability objectives. Measuring impact not only provides actionable insights for continuous improvement but also demonstrates accountability and reinforces credibility with stakeholders.

Finally, **long-term loyalty and brand equity** are strengthened through co-creation. Consumers who feel genuinely involved in shaping a brand's offerings develop a sense of ownership, commitment, and advocacy that goes beyond transactional relationships. This emotional investment fosters resilience in competitive markets, reinforces trust, and positions the brand as genuinely purpose-driven.

## Managing Risk in Partnerships

**Managing Risk in Partnerships** is a critical aspect of purpose-driven and sustainable brand strategy. As organizations increasingly collaborate with NGOs, startups, government bodies, influencers, or other external partners to amplify impact and drive innovation, the complexity and potential risks of such partnerships also rise. Effective risk management ensures that partnerships deliver mutual value, align with brand purpose, and maintain credibility while safeguarding against operational, financial, legal, reputational, and ethical challenges.

At its core, managing risk in partnerships involves **identifying, assessing, and mitigating potential threats** that could compromise the effectiveness, integrity, or sustainability of a collaboration. These risks may include misalignment of values, regulatory non-compliance, operational inefficiencies, reputational damage, data security issues, or unforeseen crises. Proactive risk management ensures that the benefits of collaboration—such as shared expertise, innovation, reach, and credibility—are realized without jeopardizing the brand's long-term objectives or stakeholder trust.

**Value and purpose alignment** are the first pillars of risk management. Before entering a partnership, brands must evaluate whether the potential partner shares compatible ethical standards, sustainability commitments, and mission-driven objectives. Misalignment can lead to conflicts, inconsistent messaging, or public backlash, particularly in purpose-driven campaigns targeting conscious consumers. Conducting thorough due diligence on the partner's history, operational practices, and public reputation reduces the likelihood of future conflicts.

**Legal and regulatory compliance** is another essential consideration. Partnerships often involve contracts, joint initiatives, and shared responsibilities that are subject to local and international laws, including labor standards, environmental regulations, and data privacy requirements. Clear contractual agreements outlining roles, responsibilities, deliverables, intellectual property rights, and liability clauses help protect all parties and mitigate legal risks. Compliance ensures that partnerships operate within ethical and legal boundaries while reinforcing accountability.

**Reputational risk management** is particularly critical in collaborations with high visibility. A partner's misconduct, public controversies, or misaligned messaging can directly impact the brand's credibility and consumer trust. Monitoring partner activities, establishing communication protocols, and preparing contingency plans enable rapid response if issues arise. Transparent communication with stakeholders during crises further safeguards reputation and demonstrates integrity.

**Operational and financial risk** must also be considered. Partnerships may face challenges such as delays, resource mismanagement, or financial instability of one party. Risk mitigation strategies include performance monitoring, clear milestones, joint governance structures, and contingency planning. By establishing accountability mechanisms and regular progress reviews, brands can maintain control over partnership outcomes and minimize operational disruptions.

**Data security and privacy risks** are particularly relevant in collaborations involving shared information, customer data, or analytics. Brands must ensure that partners adhere to robust cybersecurity standards, comply with data protection regulations, and implement protocols for secure data handling. Clear agreements on data ownership, access rights, and usage limitations help prevent breaches, misuse, or unauthorized sharing, protecting both the brand and its stakeholders.

**Cultural and interpersonal risk** also requires attention. Differences in organizational culture, communication styles, or decision-making processes can create misunderstandings or conflicts. Establishing clear channels for dialogue, conflict resolution mechanisms, and shared governance practices fosters collaboration, builds mutual trust, and reduces friction over time.

**Monitoring, evaluation, and feedback loops** strengthen risk management in partnerships. Regular assessment of performance, alignment with objectives, and stakeholder feedback allows brands to identify emerging risks early and take corrective action. Transparent reporting and mutual accountability create a culture of continuous improvement, ensuring that the partnership remains effective, ethical, and sustainable.

**Exit strategies and contingency planning** are essential safeguards. Not all partnerships succeed, and brands must plan for circumstances where disengagement becomes necessary. Clear guidelines on termination, knowledge transfer, and risk mitigation minimize disruption, protect assets, and preserve relationships, ensuring that the brand can pivot without compromising its reputation or objectives.

Finally, effective **risk management in partnerships** contributes to long-term brand resilience and trust. By proactively addressing ethical, operational, financial, legal, and reputational risks, brands ensure that collaborations strengthen purpose, credibility, and stakeholder loyalty rather than exposing the organization to avoidable harm. Partnerships that are carefully structured, monitored, and aligned with brand values can deliver transformative impact while safeguarding long-term sustainability.

# Metrics, Measurement, and Reporting

# Sustainability KPIs for Marketers

**Sustainability KPIs for Marketers** are specialized metrics that allow marketing professionals to measure, track, and communicate the environmental, social, and ethical impact of their campaigns, initiatives, and overall brand activities. Unlike traditional marketing KPIs, which focus primarily on sales, engagement, or conversion rates, sustainability KPIs integrate purpose-driven objectives, conscious consumer expectations, and long-term brand credibility into performance evaluation. By adopting these metrics, marketers can ensure that their strategies are not only effective in generating revenue but also responsible, transparent, and aligned with corporate sustainability goals.

At its core, sustainability KPIs provide **quantifiable benchmarks** that connect marketing efforts to environmental, social, and ethical outcomes. Examples include measuring reductions in carbon emissions due to digital campaigns, the proportion of recycled or sustainable materials used in product packaging, energy savings from eco-friendly initiatives, or engagement rates with purpose-driven content. These KPIs allow marketers to evaluate the tangible impact of their campaigns and communicate results to stakeholders, including consumers, investors, and internal leadership.

**Environmental KPIs** focus on the ecological footprint of marketing activities. Marketers can track metrics such as digital carbon footprint (energy consumed by online campaigns, data storage, or streaming), waste reduction from packaging or promotional materials, sustainable sourcing of marketing collateral, and adoption of eco-friendly distribution channels. By measuring these factors, brands demonstrate accountability and provide evidence that marketing activities support broader environmental objectives, such as carbon neutrality or circular economy practices.

**Social KPIs** measure the influence of marketing on communities, diversity, equity, and inclusion, and societal well-being. Metrics may include participation rates in social impact campaigns, community engagement levels, improvements in consumer awareness about ethical practices, or the reach of educational initiatives on sustainability. These KPIs help marketers quantify the societal contribution of their efforts and align campaigns with purpose-driven objectives, fostering positive consumer perception and long-term loyalty.

**Ethical and governance KPIs** assess transparency, compliance, and adherence to responsible marketing practices. Marketers can track adherence to data privacy regulations, accuracy in sustainability claims, reduction in greenwashing incidents, and levels of stakeholder trust in communications. Ethical KPIs ensure that campaigns uphold integrity, maintain consumer confidence, and reinforce the brand's credibility.

**Engagement and behavioral KPIs** measure how sustainability-oriented marketing influences consumer action. Metrics can include the number of users adopting eco-friendly behaviors, participation in cause-related campaigns, downloads of sustainability-focused apps, or conversion rates for products with environmentally responsible attributes. Tracking these behaviors allows marketers to evaluate whether campaigns are translating purpose into tangible outcomes, rather than just generating awareness.

**Brand perception KPIs** link sustainability initiatives to long-term brand equity. Marketers can assess shifts in consumer perception, trust, advocacy, and loyalty in response to purpose-driven campaigns. Surveys, sentiment analysis, net promoter scores, and social listening provide insight into how audiences perceive the brand's commitment to sustainability and ethical values, helping marketers refine strategies and messaging to reinforce alignment with conscious consumer expectations.

**Integration with ROI and traditional KPIs** ensures that sustainability measurement is actionable and relevant to business outcomes. For instance, marketers can evaluate the financial impact of sustainability campaigns by tracking incremental sales, customer acquisition, or retention associated with purpose-driven initiatives. This integrated approach demonstrates that sustainability is not separate from performance but enhances long-term growth, loyalty, and brand differentiation.

**Continuous monitoring and reporting** are essential for credibility. Sustainability KPIs should be tracked regularly, benchmarked against internal and external standards, and communicated transparently to stakeholders. Dashboards, reports, and third-party validation enhance accountability and demonstrate that the brand's marketing efforts are making measurable, meaningful contributions to environmental and social goals.

**Innovation and improvement** are driven by KPIs. By analyzing sustainability performance, marketers can identify areas for optimization—whether in campaign design, material selection, digital strategy, or community engagement. This creates a feedback loop that ensures marketing continuously evolves to reduce environmental impact, enhance social value, and strengthen ethical practices.

Finally, sustainability KPIs foster **long-term brand purpose and stakeholder trust**. Brands that track, measure, and report meaningful impact reinforce credibility, resonate with conscious consumers, and differentiate themselves in competitive markets. By demonstrating accountability and delivering quantifiable outcomes, marketers can position sustainability as a core component of strategy rather than a peripheral activity.

## Integrating Marketing and ESG Metrics

**Integrating Marketing and ESG Metrics** is a strategic approach that aligns a brand's marketing performance with its broader Environmental, Social, and Governance (ESG) objectives. In today's conscious consumer landscape, marketing is no longer just about driving sales or engagement; it is also about communicating and reinforcing a company's commitment to sustainability, ethical practices, and social responsibility. By integrating ESG metrics into marketing strategy, brands can demonstrate accountability, strengthen credibility, and ensure that campaigns contribute to both business performance and societal impact.

At its core, this integration involves **linking traditional marketing KPIs—such as reach, engagement, conversions, and ROI—to ESG outcomes**. For example, a campaign promoting eco-friendly products can track not only sales or digital engagement but also reductions in carbon footprint, use of sustainable materials, or contributions to community programs. By creating a clear connection between marketing activities and ESG goals, organizations reinforce their purpose-driven strategy and provide measurable evidence of impact.

**Environmental integration** focuses on the ecological outcomes of marketing campaigns and initiatives. Metrics can include carbon emissions associated with digital campaigns, energy consumption in marketing operations, sustainable sourcing of promotional materials, and reductions in packaging waste. Tracking these metrics alongside marketing performance ensures that communications and campaigns support the company's environmental commitments while minimizing the ecological footprint of outreach activities.

**Social integration** emphasizes marketing's role in advancing social responsibility and community impact. Metrics may include diversity and inclusion in campaigns, engagement in social initiatives, advocacy for community programs, or improvements in consumer awareness regarding social or ethical issues. By aligning marketing activities with social KPIs, brands ensure that their messaging resonates authentically with conscious consumers and supports positive societal outcomes.

**Governance integration** addresses transparency, accountability, and ethical standards in marketing practices. This includes adherence to data privacy regulations, accuracy in sustainability claims, reduction of misleading messaging, and alignment with corporate governance policies. Marketing teams that integrate governance metrics demonstrate ethical responsibility, mitigate reputational risks, and build trust with consumers, investors, and other stakeholders.

**Cross-functional collaboration** is essential for successful integration. Marketing teams must work closely with ESG, sustainability, and compliance departments to ensure that metrics are aligned, reporting is accurate, and campaigns reflect true organizational commitments. Collaboration ensures that ESG goals are not siloed but embedded into all stages of campaign design, execution, and evaluation.

**Measurement frameworks** should combine quantitative and qualitative indicators. Quantitative metrics, such as energy savings, waste reduction, or social program participation, provide concrete evidence of ESG impact. Qualitative metrics, such as stakeholder sentiment, community feedback, or brand perception regarding sustainability and ethics, provide insights into the effectiveness of purpose-driven messaging. Together, they offer a holistic view of how marketing contributes to ESG objectives.

**Transparency and reporting** enhance credibility. Brands should communicate both marketing results and ESG impact to stakeholders in a clear, accessible, and verifiable manner. Dashboards, sustainability reports, and campaign summaries can highlight how marketing efforts support environmental, social, and governance goals, fostering trust and reinforcing authenticity. Third-party validation or certification of ESG claims further strengthens stakeholder confidence.

**Optimization and continuous improvement** are facilitated by integrating marketing and ESG metrics. By monitoring performance, identifying gaps, and evaluating the ESG implications of campaigns, marketers can adjust strategies to improve both commercial outcomes and social or environmental impact. This iterative process ensures that marketing remains aligned with evolving sustainability standards and stakeholder expectations.

**Competitive differentiation** is another benefit. Brands that successfully demonstrate the tangible ESG impact of their marketing campaigns differentiate themselves in the marketplace. Conscious consumers, investors, and partners increasingly reward organizations that embed sustainability and ethical responsibility into every aspect of their operations, including communications and marketing.

**Long-term brand value** is reinforced through this integration. Aligning marketing with ESG metrics ensures that campaigns not only drive immediate results but also strengthen credibility, loyalty, and advocacy. Consumers perceive the brand as authentic, trustworthy, and purpose-driven, leading to sustained engagement and resilience in competitive markets.

## Tools for Impact Measurement

**Tools for Impact Measurement** are essential for marketers, sustainability professionals, and business leaders seeking to quantify, track, and communicate the effectiveness of purpose-driven initiatives. In a conscious consumer and ESG-focused world, it is no longer sufficient to measure campaigns and strategies solely through traditional metrics such as sales, clicks, or engagement. Tools for impact measurement allow organizations to evaluate the environmental, social, and governance (ESG) outcomes of their activities, ensure accountability, optimize strategies, and demonstrate credibility to stakeholders.

At the core, impact measurement tools provide **structured methodologies and technological capabilities** to collect, analyze, and report data on a wide range of outcomes. They enable organizations to move beyond anecdotal or qualitative assessments, offering rigorous, data-backed insights into how marketing campaigns, corporate initiatives, or sustainability programs affect both business objectives and societal outcomes. These tools help quantify results in areas such as carbon emissions reduction, social engagement, community benefits, ethical compliance, and resource efficiency.

**Digital analytics platforms** are among the most widely used tools for measuring impact in marketing and ESG initiatives. Tools like Google Analytics, Adobe Analytics, and social media insights dashboards track engagement, reach, conversions, and audience behavior. When combined with purpose-driven objectives, these platforms can provide insights into how sustainability messaging resonates with audiences, which campaigns drive conscious consumer action, and how digital initiatives affect resource consumption or carbon footprint.

**Sustainability assessment and reporting tools** focus specifically on environmental and social impact. Platforms such as EcoVadis, GRESB, CDP, and Sphera enable organizations to measure carbon emissions, energy use, water consumption, waste generation, and supply chain sustainability. These tools provide standardized frameworks for assessing ESG performance, benchmarking against industry standards, and generating credible reports for stakeholders, investors, and regulators.

**Life Cycle Assessment (LCA) tools** are critical for evaluating the environmental impact of products, campaigns, or operations across their entire lifecycle. Tools like GaBi, SimaPro, and OpenLCA allow brands to analyze material sourcing, production, distribution, usage, and end-of-life disposal, providing a comprehensive picture of ecological footprint. LCA data informs product design, packaging decisions, and marketing claims, ensuring that initiatives are grounded in measurable sustainability outcomes.

**Social impact measurement platforms** help quantify community, employee, and societal benefits. Tools such as Social Value International's framework, B Lab Impact Assessment, and SROI (Social Return on Investment) tools allow organizations to evaluate the outcomes of social programs, volunteer initiatives, and cause-driven campaigns. These platforms help marketers understand how campaigns contribute to behavioral change, social engagement, or community development, translating qualitative impact into measurable indicators.

**ESG reporting and dashboard tools** integrate multiple metrics into a centralized platform for monitoring, visualization, and decision-making. Tools like Salesforce Sustainability Cloud, Microsoft Cloud for Sustainability, and SAP Sustainability Control Tower provide dashboards that combine financial, environmental, and social KPIs.

These platforms allow marketers and executives to track performance, identify trends, and communicate results to stakeholders in a transparent and visually compelling way.

**Survey and feedback tools** are critical for capturing qualitative and perceptual data. Tools like SurveyMonkey, Typeform, and Qualtrics enable organizations to gather consumer sentiment, employee perspectives, and community feedback. Insights from these surveys complement quantitative metrics, providing context, validating impact, and informing improvements in campaigns or programs.

**Third-party verification and certification tools** add credibility to impact measurement. Organizations often leverage independent audits, certification programs, and industry standards—such as ISO 14001 (environmental management), Fair Trade, or LEED certification—to verify claims and ensure accountability. Third-party validation reduces skepticism, enhances trust, and ensures that reported impact aligns with recognized benchmarks.

**Data visualization and storytelling tools** enhance communication of impact. Platforms like Tableau, Power BI, and Google Data Studio allow marketers to create clear, interactive dashboards that illustrate environmental, social, and governance outcomes alongside traditional marketing metrics. Effective visualization helps stakeholders understand the tangible results of initiatives, driving engagement, transparency, and credibility.

**Integration and automation tools** enable seamless aggregation of impact data across multiple systems. APIs, CRM integrations, and workflow automation allow marketers to consolidate campaign performance, ESG metrics, and operational data into unified dashboards. This ensures real-time monitoring, reduces errors, and facilitates strategic decision-making.

Finally, **continuous monitoring and improvement frameworks** are essential for ensuring that measurement tools drive actionable insights. Combining quantitative data, qualitative feedback, and benchmarking enables brands to optimize campaigns, refine sustainability strategies, and enhance long-term impact. Tools alone are insufficient without structured processes for analysis, decision-making, and reporting.

## Reporting Standards and Compliance

**Reporting Standards and Compliance** are essential components of purpose-driven and sustainability-focused marketing and business strategy. As brands increasingly integrate Environmental, Social, and Governance (ESG) initiatives into their operations, stakeholders—from conscious consumers to investors and regulators—demand transparency, accountability, and credible disclosure of impact. Reporting standards provide a structured framework for measuring and communicating performance, while compliance ensures that these disclosures are accurate, consistent, and aligned with legal and ethical obligations. Together, they enhance trust, credibility, and long-term brand value.

At the core, **reporting standards** define the metrics, methodologies, and formats that organizations should use when disclosing ESG and sustainability information. They ensure consistency across industries and geographies, enabling stakeholders to compare performance meaningfully. Common reporting frameworks include the Global Reporting Initiative (GRI), Sustainability Accounting Standards Board (SASB), Task Force on Climate-related Financial Disclosures (TCFD), and Integrated Reporting (IR). Each framework focuses on specific dimensions—environmental impact, social responsibility, governance, or financial integration—helping brands structure disclosures in a comprehensive and credible manner.

**Environmental reporting standards** focus on quantifying a company's ecological footprint and sustainability practices. Metrics often include greenhouse gas emissions, energy consumption, water usage, waste management, and resource efficiency. Frameworks such as GRI and CDP (formerly Carbon Disclosure Project) provide detailed guidelines for measurement and reporting, ensuring that environmental claims are transparent, standardized, and verifiable. Accurate environmental reporting is critical for brands pursuing climate goals, carbon neutrality, or sustainable product initiatives.

**Social reporting standards** evaluate a company's impact on employees, communities, customers, and broader society. Metrics may include labor practices, diversity and inclusion, employee well-being, human rights compliance, and community development initiatives. Adhering to social reporting standards ensures that brands provide verifiable information about their contributions to social responsibility, fostering credibility and engagement with conscious consumers and stakeholders.

**Governance reporting standards** address the ethical, legal, and strategic oversight of business operations. Metrics often include board composition, executive compensation, risk management processes, anti-corruption measures, and transparency in decision-making. Governance disclosures, guided by frameworks like SASB and TCFD, demonstrate that the brand operates with integrity, accountability, and strategic foresight, which is increasingly important to investors and regulatory bodies.

**Compliance** ensures that reporting aligns with legal, regulatory, and industry requirements. Non-compliance can lead to legal penalties, reputational damage, or loss of stakeholder trust. Compliance requires organizations to maintain accurate records, implement verification processes, and adhere to disclosure deadlines. It also involves integrating ESG reporting with financial reporting in jurisdictions where regulations mandate transparency, such as the EU Corporate Sustainability Reporting Directive (CSRD) or the SEC's climate disclosure rules in the United States.

**Materiality assessment** is a critical element in reporting and compliance. Brands must identify which ESG issues are most relevant to their business operations and stakeholders, ensuring that disclosures are focused on significant impacts rather than superficial metrics. This prioritization enhances credibility, reduces reporting burden, and ensures that reporting provides meaningful insights rather than generic statements.

**Third-party verification and assurance** further strengthen compliance and credibility. Independent audits or certifications validate the accuracy of reported data and adherence to reporting standards. Assurance providers examine methodologies, data sources, and disclosures to ensure that reports are reliable, transparent, and free from misrepresentation. Third-party validation is particularly important for sustainability claims, where stakeholder skepticism is high.

**Digital tools and reporting platforms** facilitate compliance and efficiency. Systems such as SAP Sustainability Control Tower, Salesforce Sustainability Cloud, and Enablon help collect, standardize, and visualize ESG data, enabling real-time tracking, benchmarking, and reporting. These platforms support alignment with multiple reporting frameworks simultaneously, streamlining processes and reducing the risk of errors.

**Stakeholder communication** is an integral part of reporting standards. Effective reporting not only ensures compliance but also communicates impact to consumers, investors, employees, and partners in a clear, transparent, and engaging manner. Visual dashboards, sustainability reports, and interactive platforms allow stakeholders to understand progress, assess performance, and make informed decisions based on credible data.

**Continuous improvement and iterative reporting** are essential. Reporting is not a one-time activity but an ongoing process that allows brands to track progress, identify gaps, and refine strategies. By integrating lessons learned and feedback from stakeholders, organizations can enhance both the quality of disclosures and the effectiveness of sustainability initiatives over time.

Finally, adherence to reporting standards and compliance reinforces **brand credibility, trust, and long-term value**. Brands that consistently disclose accurate, verified, and material ESG information demonstrate accountability, authenticity, and leadership in purpose-driven practices. This transparency strengthens relationships with conscious consumers, investors, regulators, and partners, creating a competitive advantage in a market where ethical and sustainable practices are increasingly valued.

# Turning Data into Strategic Action

**Turning Data into Strategic Action** is a critical capability for modern marketers and business leaders, particularly in a conscious consumer and sustainability-focused environment. Collecting data—whether on consumer behavior, ESG performance, campaign effectiveness, or social engagement—is only the first step. The real value lies in translating this data into actionable insights that inform strategy, optimize decision-making, drive purpose-driven impact, and enhance long-term brand value. This approach ensures that marketing, operational, and sustainability initiatives are evidence-based, measurable, and aligned with organizational objectives.

At the core, turning data into strategic action involves **collecting relevant, high-quality data, analyzing it systematically, and integrating insights into decision-making processes**. For marketers, this includes traditional performance metrics such as engagement, conversion rates, and ROI, alongside sustainability-related data, such as carbon footprint of campaigns, ethical sourcing metrics, social impact outcomes, and consumer sentiment toward purpose-driven initiatives. The ability to combine these datasets allows organizations to understand not only what is happening but why, and what adjustments are necessary to improve results.

**Data aggregation and integration** are foundational steps. Organizations often have data scattered across multiple systems, from CRM platforms and social analytics tools to sustainability dashboards and financial reporting systems. Centralizing and integrating these data sources ensures a holistic view of performance across marketing, ESG, and operational domains. Tools like Tableau, Power BI, and Salesforce Sustainability Cloud enable visualization and correlation of diverse datasets, making patterns and insights more accessible to decision-makers.

**Advanced analytics and AI-driven insights** transform raw data into actionable intelligence. Techniques such as predictive analytics, machine learning, and sentiment analysis allow brands to anticipate consumer behavior, identify trends, optimize campaigns, and forecast outcomes. For example, predictive models can highlight which sustainability messages are most likely to influence conscious consumer behavior, or which supply chain initiatives will deliver the greatest environmental benefit. By leveraging these advanced analytics, organizations can move from reactive reporting to proactive strategy formulation.

**Prioritization and decision-making** are essential aspects of turning data into strategic action. Not all data points are equally important; organizations must identify high-impact metrics that align with both business objectives and sustainability goals. Materiality assessments help focus attention on critical ESG or marketing performance areas, ensuring that strategic decisions address the most significant opportunities and risks. This prevents data overload and ensures that efforts are targeted and efficient.

**Scenario planning and testing** enhance strategic use of data. By modeling different options, simulating outcomes, and testing small-scale initiatives, brands can make informed choices before full-scale implementation. For instance, a company may pilot a sustainable packaging campaign with select consumer segments, analyze engagement and behavioral outcomes, and then scale based on data-driven insights. This iterative approach minimizes risk while maximizing impact.

**Cross-functional collaboration** ensures that insights are translated into coordinated action. Marketing, sustainability, operations, finance, and strategy teams must work together to interpret data, define objectives, and implement initiatives. By breaking down silos, organizations ensure that insights from ESG performance, consumer behavior, or operational efficiency inform decisions across departments, creating alignment and synergy between purpose-driven goals and business outcomes.

**Feedback loops and continuous improvement** are vital for sustaining strategic action. Data should be continuously monitored, with results compared against objectives and benchmarks. Insights gleaned from campaigns or initiatives should feed back into planning, allowing adjustments to messaging, processes, or resource allocation. Continuous learning ensures that strategies evolve with consumer expectations, market trends, and sustainability standards.

**Transparency and communication** amplify the impact of data-driven strategies. Sharing insights with stakeholders—internally and externally—demonstrates accountability, reinforces credibility, and fosters engagement. For example, reporting data-driven improvements in sustainability initiatives or purpose-driven campaigns to consumers, investors, or employees strengthens trust and showcases the organization's commitment to measurable, positive impact.

**Measurement of outcomes and impact** is critical. Strategic action is only meaningful if it leads to observable improvements in business performance, consumer engagement, or societal outcomes. KPIs and ESG metrics must be tracked alongside traditional marketing measures to evaluate whether data-informed decisions are achieving desired results. Metrics such as customer adoption of sustainable products, reductions in carbon emissions, increased engagement in social initiatives, or improvement in brand trust reflect the success of data-driven strategies.

Finally, turning data into strategic action strengthens **long-term brand resilience and purpose alignment**. Organizations that effectively leverage data to guide marketing, operational, and sustainability initiatives demonstrate accountability, authenticity, and strategic foresight. Data-driven decisions ensure that brands are not only responsive to market trends but also proactive in creating meaningful societal and environmental impact, building trust and loyalty among conscious consumers.

# Global Markets and Local Responsibility

# Sustainability Across Diverse Markets

**Sustainability Across Diverse Markets** explores how brands can effectively implement purpose-driven, sustainable strategies in regions with differing cultural, economic, social, and regulatory contexts. In a globalized marketplace, conscious consumer expectations, environmental challenges, and governance standards vary widely across geographies. To remain relevant, credible, and impactful, organizations must adapt sustainability initiatives to resonate with local priorities while maintaining consistency with overarching brand values. Successfully navigating these variations allows brands to achieve both social and commercial objectives on a global scale.

At the core, sustainability across diverse markets requires **understanding local consumer values and priorities**. While environmental consciousness may drive purchasing behavior in one market, social equity, fair labor practices, or economic development may be more relevant in another. For instance, consumers in Scandinavian countries may prioritize carbon-neutral products and energy efficiency, while emerging markets may place greater emphasis on job creation, affordability, and community development. Brands must research and segment markets to identify the sustainability factors that influence behavior, loyalty, and advocacy in each region.

**Cultural sensitivity** is essential. Sustainability is not a one-size-fits-all concept; how environmental or social initiatives are communicated can determine their effectiveness. Messaging, imagery, and campaigns must resonate with local norms, values, and languages to avoid misinterpretation or backlash. A campaign emphasizing minimalist consumption may be celebrated in some regions but could be perceived as impractical or irrelevant in others. Local adaptation ensures that sustainability narratives feel authentic, respectful, and relatable to each audience.

**Regulatory and compliance considerations** also shape sustainable strategies across markets. Environmental regulations, labor laws, reporting requirements, and consumer protection standards differ significantly between countries and regions. Brands must ensure that products, supply chains, and marketing practices comply with local legislation while meeting global sustainability commitments. Alignment with both local and international standards mitigates legal risks, reinforces credibility, and demonstrates responsible corporate behavior.

**Supply chain adaptation** is critical for global sustainability. Sourcing materials, manufacturing, and distribution practices must account for local environmental conditions, labor practices, and resource availability. In some markets, sourcing sustainably may involve partnerships with local farmers or suppliers to reduce environmental impact and support economic development. In others, advanced technologies or certifications may be necessary to meet regulatory or consumer expectations. Tailoring supply chain practices ensures that sustainability initiatives are feasible, effective, and locally relevant.

**Economic and infrastructural factors** influence sustainability adoption. Developing markets may face challenges such as limited access to renewable energy, recycling infrastructure, or sustainable materials. Brands operating in these contexts must innovate solutions that balance environmental goals with affordability and practicality. Conversely, in developed markets with strong infrastructure, brands can implement advanced sustainability initiatives, such as circular economy models, smart packaging, or carbon-neutral logistics, to meet higher consumer and regulatory expectations.

**Partnerships and stakeholder engagement** enhance local relevance. Collaborating with NGOs, government agencies, startups, and community organizations helps brands understand local sustainability priorities, co-create initiatives, and achieve meaningful impact. These partnerships provide expertise, credibility, and networks that facilitate the adaptation of global sustainability objectives to diverse regional contexts.

**Monitoring and reporting** must account for regional differences while maintaining global consistency. ESG metrics, sustainability KPIs, and impact reporting should reflect local outcomes and challenges, providing a nuanced understanding of performance across markets. Simultaneously, aggregated reporting ensures that global stakeholders—including investors and corporate leadership—receive a coherent picture of the brand's overall sustainability efforts.

**Consumer education and engagement** are key to adoption. In markets where sustainability awareness is nascent, brands may need to invest in campaigns that educate consumers about eco-friendly practices, ethical sourcing, or social responsibility. In contrast, markets with highly conscious consumers may require initiatives that demonstrate leadership, innovation, and measurable impact. Tailoring engagement strategies ensures that consumers across diverse markets understand, value, and participate in sustainability initiatives.

**Balancing global consistency with local adaptation** is a strategic challenge. Brands must ensure that their sustainability vision, values, and commitments remain consistent worldwide while allowing flexibility to respond to local contexts. This balance fosters credibility, prevents brand dilution, and ensures that initiatives are both meaningful and achievable in each market.

Finally, **long-term brand equity and competitive advantage** are strengthened through effective sustainability across diverse markets. By respecting cultural differences, complying with local regulations, adapting supply chains, and engaging stakeholders meaningfully, brands build trust, loyalty, and advocacy globally. Conscious consumers recognize and reward companies that demonstrate both authenticity and adaptability, reinforcing market leadership and resilience.

# Localization Without Compromising Values

**Localization Without Compromising Values** refers to the strategic approach of adapting marketing, products, and sustainability initiatives to local markets while remaining true to a brand's core purpose, ethical principles, and global values. In an increasingly interconnected world, brands operate across diverse geographies, cultures, and regulatory landscapes. Consumers expect relevance, cultural sensitivity, and practical solutions, yet they also demand authenticity and integrity. Successfully balancing localization with consistent values allows brands to resonate with local audiences without diluting purpose or credibility.

At the core, localization involves **tailoring products, campaigns, messaging, and operations** to meet the specific needs, preferences, and constraints of a regional market. This may include language adaptation, cultural references, regulatory compliance, pricing strategies, or distribution methods. For example, a sustainable fashion brand may use locally sourced materials and regional artisans in one country, while in another market it may emphasize circular supply chains or eco-friendly production technologies. Both approaches achieve sustainability goals, but each is tailored to local realities and consumer expectations.

**Preserving core values** is essential when localizing. Brands must clearly define their guiding principles—such as environmental stewardship, ethical sourcing, inclusivity, and transparency—and ensure that every local adaptation aligns with these values. Compromising on these fundamentals may provide short-term market gains but can erode credibility, consumer trust, and long-term brand equity. Authenticity is the bridge between local relevance and global integrity; consumers increasingly scrutinize whether a brand's local actions truly reflect its stated mission and ethics.

**Cultural sensitivity** is a key aspect of localization. Understanding local traditions, social norms, and communication styles ensures that campaigns are effective and respectful. Sustainability messaging, for example, may emphasize energy conservation in one region and community development in another, depending on what resonates most with local audiences. By respecting cultural context, brands avoid misinterpretation, backlash, or perceptions of superficiality, while still reinforcing overarching values.

**Regulatory compliance and local governance** are integral to successful localization. Different regions impose unique environmental, labor, and business regulations. Adapting operations and reporting practices to comply with local law ensures legal integrity while demonstrating responsible corporate behavior. For instance, a brand may implement different packaging requirements or emissions reporting standards across countries while maintaining the same commitment to environmental sustainability globally.

**Supply chain adaptation** is another critical dimension. Local sourcing, partnerships with regional suppliers, or adoption of region-specific technologies can enhance sustainability outcomes while improving relevance and efficiency. However, these adaptations must not compromise ethical standards, labor practices, or environmental commitments. Clear guidelines and rigorous monitoring ensure that localized supply chains remain aligned with global values.

**Consumer engagement and communication** must balance relatability with authenticity. Messaging should reflect local realities, preferences, and priorities while remaining consistent with the brand's purpose. Storytelling, campaigns, and educational initiatives can be tailored to address local challenges or highlight regional success stories without contradicting global principles. This approach ensures that consumers perceive the brand as both relevant and principled.

**Training and empowerment of local teams** are essential to uphold values in diverse markets. Employees and partners who understand the brand's global mission, ethical standards, and sustainability objectives can make informed decisions about localized actions. Clear guidelines, communication protocols, and continuous education ensure alignment and prevent inadvertent compromise of core values during local execution.

**Monitoring, feedback, and continuous improvement** help maintain balance between localization and value preservation. Brands must track local performance against both business and sustainability KPIs, ensuring that adaptations are effective and ethically sound. Stakeholder feedback—from consumers, partners, and community organizations—provides insights into whether localized actions are perceived as authentic and impactful, allowing for course corrections when necessary.

**Balancing flexibility and consistency** is the strategic principle underlying localization without compromising values. While execution can vary to fit regional needs, the underlying ethical commitments, purpose-driven objectives, and sustainability standards remain constant. This dual approach allows brands to be culturally and operationally agile without losing credibility or diluting their mission.

Finally, **long-term brand equity and trust** benefit from this balance. Brands that successfully localize while maintaining integrity strengthen relationships with conscious consumers, investors, and communities. They demonstrate that purpose is not a rigid slogan but a living framework that adapts intelligently to context, enhancing resilience, relevance, and global leadership.

## Emerging Markets and Inclusive Growth

**Emerging Markets and Inclusive Growth** explores how brands can expand sustainably into fast-growing economies while promoting equitable economic, social, and environmental development. Emerging markets—characterized by rapid urbanization, expanding consumer bases, and evolving regulatory frameworks—present both tremendous opportunity and responsibility. For conscious, purpose-driven brands, success in these markets requires strategies that not only drive business growth but also contribute to inclusive development, empower communities, and foster long-term resilience.

At its core, **inclusive growth** means ensuring that economic gains are broadly shared across all segments of society, including marginalized populations, small businesses, and underserved communities. For brands entering emerging markets, this principle involves designing products, services, and initiatives that address local needs, improve accessibility, and create opportunities for employment, education, and skill development. Inclusive growth aligns business objectives with social impact, reinforcing the brand's purpose and credibility.

**Understanding the socio-economic landscape** is critical. Emerging markets often face challenges such as income inequality, limited infrastructure, and resource constraints, alongside unique cultural, regulatory, and environmental contexts. Brands must conduct deep market research to understand consumer behavior, local priorities, and systemic barriers to access. This knowledge informs strategies that are both commercially viable and socially responsible. For example, a consumer goods company may develop affordable, sustainably produced products tailored to low-income segments while simultaneously supporting local supply chains and small-scale producers.

**Local partnerships** play a central role in promoting inclusive growth. Collaborations with NGOs, startups, community organizations, and government agencies help brands design initiatives that have meaningful, scalable impact. Such partnerships provide access to local expertise, networks, and resources that are essential for understanding community needs and implementing programs that empower stakeholders. For instance, a brand working in renewable energy could partner with local cooperatives to provide solar solutions to underserved communities, creating both environmental and social benefits.

**Employment and skills development** are key drivers of inclusive growth. Brands can contribute by creating job opportunities, supporting vocational training, and building local capacities within emerging markets. These efforts not only improve livelihoods but also strengthen supply chains and community engagement. For example, a fashion brand sourcing from emerging markets may train local artisans in sustainable practices, improving product quality, ensuring fair wages, and promoting long-term economic development.

**Sustainable and affordable innovation** is crucial in these markets. Products and services should be designed to meet local needs, optimize resource use, and reduce environmental impact. Affordable sustainability ensures that conscious consumerism is not limited to high-income segments but accessible to a broader population. Brands that innovate with inclusivity in mind—such as low-cost renewable energy, eco-friendly household goods, or community-focused financial services—can drive both market growth and social progress simultaneously.

**Regulatory engagement and compliance** are essential in emerging markets. These economies often have evolving legal frameworks regarding labor standards, environmental protection, and business practices. Brands that proactively align with local regulations and contribute to policy development demonstrate responsible corporate citizenship. Regulatory compliance ensures legal integrity while reinforcing stakeholder trust, particularly among conscious consumers and investors concerned with ESG performance.

**Community engagement and empowerment** amplify impact. Brands that actively involve local communities in co-creation, decision-making, and program implementation enhance relevance, ownership, and long-term success. Engagement can take the form of consumer education, participatory product design, or social initiatives addressing local priorities. Such approaches foster trust, loyalty, and advocacy, while ensuring that growth benefits are widely shared.

**Measuring impact and accountability** is critical for demonstrating inclusive growth. Brands must track both business and social outcomes, such as economic opportunities created, environmental improvements, and community participation rates. Transparent reporting and third-party verification build credibility and allow continuous improvement, ensuring that strategies deliver tangible benefits while reinforcing purpose-driven messaging.

**Balancing scale and ethical responsibility** is a strategic challenge. While emerging markets offer significant growth potential, rapid expansion without attention to inclusivity and sustainability can lead to exploitation, resource depletion, or reputational damage. Purpose-driven brands must integrate ESG principles into market entry strategies, supply chains, marketing, and operations, ensuring that growth is responsible, equitable, and sustainable.

Finally, **long-term brand equity and competitive advantage** are strengthened through inclusive growth in emerging markets. Companies that demonstrate commitment to social, economic, and environmental well-being earn trust, loyalty, and advocacy from local communities, conscious consumers, and global stakeholders. Inclusive growth reinforces the brand's purpose, builds resilience against market volatility, and positions the organization as a leader in both profitability and societal impact.

## Cultural Sensitivity in Sustainable Messaging

**Cultural Sensitivity in Sustainable Messaging** is a crucial component of purpose-driven marketing, particularly in today's globalized and diverse marketplace. As brands communicate their sustainability initiatives, environmental commitments, and social impact efforts, they must ensure that messaging resonates across different cultures, values, and social norms without alienating or offending any audience. Cultural sensitivity ensures that sustainability narratives are relevant, authentic, and effective, while preserving the credibility and ethical integrity of the brand.

At its core, cultural sensitivity involves **understanding local beliefs, traditions, social priorities, and communication preferences**. Sustainability is interpreted differently across regions: what resonates as urgent or meaningful in one culture may be trivial or even inappropriate in another. For example, campaigns emphasizing water conservation may be compelling in regions facing drought, while emphasizing plastic reduction may be more impactful in coastal areas affected by pollution. Tailoring messaging to cultural context ensures that sustainability initiatives are perceived as relevant, credible, and actionable.

**Language and tone** are essential aspects of culturally sensitive messaging. Words, metaphors, and imagery can carry different connotations across languages and societies. Brands must carefully choose messaging that avoids misinterpretation, stereotyping, or offense. For instance, emphasizing "minimalism" in a culture where abundance symbolizes prosperity may be misaligned; instead, framing sustainability as innovation, efficiency, or community well-being may resonate more effectively. Proper localization without losing the core sustainability message is a delicate but critical balance.

**Cultural values and priorities** influence how sustainability is perceived. Some societies prioritize environmental conservation, while others may emphasize social equity, labor rights, or economic development. Understanding these local values allows brands to craft messaging that highlights aspects of sustainability most relevant to the audience. For example, campaigns focused on ethical labor practices may resonate strongly in regions with historical exploitation, while carbon reduction or renewable energy initiatives may resonate in environmentally conscious markets.

**Visual and symbolic representation** also requires sensitivity. Imagery used in sustainable campaigns—whether depicting nature, communities, or product use—must be culturally appropriate and respectful. Symbols, colors, or scenarios can have varied interpretations; what represents harmony in one culture may carry negative associations in another. Cultural vetting of visual assets ensures that campaigns are inclusive and respectful, avoiding unintended backlash.

**Engagement strategies** must be adapted to cultural norms. In some regions, sustainability initiatives may be best communicated through community leaders, local influencers, or participatory campaigns that empower audiences. In others, digital storytelling, social media campaigns, or educational content may be more effective. Understanding how people communicate, engage, and make decisions culturally allows brands to design campaigns that not only inform but also motivate action.

**Inclusivity and diversity** are central to culturally sensitive sustainability messaging. Brands should reflect the diversity of the communities they serve in their campaigns, avoiding tokenism or exclusion. Inclusive messaging builds trust, strengthens relevance, and demonstrates that the brand's sustainability efforts genuinely consider all stakeholders. It also reinforces the brand's commitment to ethical and social responsibility, which is increasingly important to conscious consumers.

**Avoiding cultural assumptions and biases** is critical. Brands must not project global or Western-centric ideas of sustainability onto all markets, as this can lead to misalignment or rejection. Conducting local research, involving regional experts, and listening to community voices ensures that messaging is grounded in authentic understanding rather than assumptions. Co-creation with local stakeholders can further enhance credibility and effectiveness.

**Consistency with brand values** is essential while adapting messaging culturally. While the tone, visuals, and emphasis may vary by region, the core principles of sustainability, ethical responsibility, and purpose-driven commitment must remain consistent. This balance ensures that the brand maintains global integrity while effectively engaging diverse audiences.

**Monitoring and feedback** reinforce cultural sensitivity. Tracking audience responses, social sentiment, and engagement metrics helps brands assess whether messaging is resonating appropriately. Feedback loops allow for timely adjustments, mitigating risks of misunderstanding or cultural misalignment while optimizing the impact of sustainability campaigns.

Finally, culturally sensitive sustainability messaging strengthens **brand trust, loyalty, and long-term impact**. When consumers perceive that a brand respects their values, communicates authentically, and tailors sustainability initiatives to local priorities, it builds credibility, drives engagement, and fosters advocacy. This approach ensures that sustainability messaging is not only effective but also ethical, inclusive, and globally resonant.

## Managing Global Supply Chain Complexity

**Managing Global Supply Chain Complexity** is a critical aspect of sustainable marketing and responsible business operations in today's interconnected, conscious consumer-driven marketplace. Modern supply chains span multiple countries, suppliers, regulatory environments, and logistical networks, creating both opportunities and risks. For purpose-driven brands, complexity is not merely operational—it directly impacts sustainability, ethical compliance, brand credibility, and consumer trust. Effective management of global supply chains requires integrating operational efficiency with environmental, social, and governance (ESG) considerations while navigating the challenges of scale, diversity, and uncertainty.

At the core, global supply chain complexity arises from **geographical dispersion, diverse regulatory frameworks, and varying operational capabilities**. Brands source raw materials from multiple regions, often involving multiple tiers of suppliers, each with distinct environmental practices, labor standards, and compliance levels. Complexity is further increased by transportation networks, cross-border regulations, geopolitical factors, and evolving consumer expectations for sustainability and transparency. Failure to manage these factors can result in reputational damage, regulatory penalties, operational disruptions, and compromised brand integrity.

**Supply chain mapping and visibility** are fundamental to managing complexity. Brands must understand every tier of their supply chain, from raw material sourcing to final product delivery. Advanced mapping tools, blockchain technology, and digital dashboards enable real-time tracking of materials, labor conditions, carbon emissions, and sustainability compliance across suppliers. Visibility allows brands to identify high-risk areas, monitor performance, and ensure that ethical and environmental standards are upheld consistently across all regions.

**Supplier evaluation and collaboration** are key strategies. Assessing suppliers for compliance with environmental standards, labor practices, and social responsibility ensures that the brand's values are maintained throughout the supply chain. Collaborating with suppliers through training programs, audits, and joint sustainability initiatives fosters alignment, enhances operational performance, and drives shared value. For instance, a brand might support local suppliers in adopting renewable energy, sustainable materials, or waste reduction practices, improving both supply chain resilience and ESG performance.

**Risk management and mitigation** are critical for navigating global supply chain complexity. Brands face operational risks such as natural disasters, geopolitical disruptions, regulatory changes, and transportation bottlenecks. They also face reputational risks if suppliers engage in unethical or environmentally harmful practices. Risk mitigation strategies include diversifying suppliers, implementing contingency plans, auditing and monitoring programs, and maintaining strong contractual agreements that define sustainability and ethical expectations. Proactive risk management reduces the likelihood of disruptions and protects brand reputation.

**Technology and data analytics** play an increasingly important role. Digital platforms enable predictive modeling, scenario analysis, and real-time monitoring of supply chain performance. Artificial intelligence (AI) can optimize logistics, forecast demand, identify inefficiencies, and detect anomalies that could compromise sustainability or ethical compliance. Leveraging technology allows brands to manage complexity systematically, anticipate challenges, and implement corrective measures efficiently.

**Sustainability integration** ensures that operational decisions reflect broader ESG objectives. This includes minimizing carbon emissions through optimized logistics, adopting circular economy practices, sourcing responsibly, reducing waste, and ensuring fair labor conditions. Sustainable supply chain management not only meets regulatory and consumer expectations but also enhances long-term competitiveness and brand value. Consumers increasingly reward brands that demonstrate responsibility and accountability across their supply chains.

**Regulatory compliance** across multiple jurisdictions adds another layer of complexity. Each country may have distinct environmental laws, labor regulations, trade restrictions, and reporting requirements. Brands must ensure that all suppliers comply with these local regulations while adhering to global ESG commitments. Compliance minimizes legal risks, prevents fines or sanctions, and strengthens credibility with conscious consumers and investors.

**Stakeholder engagement** is essential. Transparency with consumers, investors, NGOs, and industry partners builds trust and demonstrates accountability. Brands can report on supplier practices, environmental impact, and social initiatives through sustainability reports, ESG disclosures, and digital dashboards. Engaging stakeholders fosters collaboration, encourages continuous improvement, and enhances the perceived authenticity of sustainability efforts.

**Continuous improvement and innovation** are critical to managing complexity sustainably. Brands must adapt supply chain strategies in response to changing consumer expectations, technological advances, and emerging sustainability standards. Innovations such as green logistics, renewable energy integration, eco-friendly packaging, and supplier capacity building can improve efficiency, reduce environmental impact, and enhance resilience.

Finally, effective management of global supply chain complexity strengthens **long-term brand resilience, competitiveness, and stakeholder trust**. Brands that successfully balance operational efficiency with sustainability and ethical responsibility can navigate disruptions, differentiate themselves in crowded markets, and demonstrate genuine purpose. Conscious consumers, investors, and partners increasingly favor organizations that manage complexity responsibly, rewarding brands with loyalty, advocacy, and long-term growth.

# Case Studies of Sustainable Marketing Excellence

# Consumer Brands Leading Sustainability

**Consumer Brands Leading Sustainability** explores how leading companies are integrating environmental, social, and ethical responsibility into their core business strategies, transforming sustainability from a peripheral initiative into a central driver of brand identity, growth, and competitive advantage. In today's conscious consumer landscape, consumers increasingly reward brands that demonstrate measurable commitment to sustainability, and leading brands are setting benchmarks for transparency, innovation, and impact. Examining how these brands operate provides critical insights into best practices, challenges, and opportunities for embedding sustainability into consumer-facing businesses.

At the core, **leading consumer brands embed sustainability into their purpose and values** rather than treating it as a marketing add-on. These brands align products, packaging, supply chains, marketing communications, and operations with clearly defined sustainability goals. This holistic approach ensures that every aspect of the consumer experience reflects ethical and environmental responsibility, reinforcing credibility and long-term trust. For example, companies in sectors such as apparel, personal care, and food are committing to circular economy principles, carbon neutrality, and ethical sourcing, making sustainability a tangible part of the brand story.

**Product innovation** is a key area where consumer brands demonstrate leadership. Sustainable brands invest in research and development to create products with lower environmental impact, enhanced durability, or ethically sourced materials. Innovations include biodegradable packaging, plant-based ingredients, energy-efficient appliances, and reusable or refillable products. By prioritizing eco-friendly design, these brands not only meet consumer demand for responsible products but also differentiate themselves in competitive markets.

**Supply chain leadership** is another defining characteristic. Leading brands proactively assess and manage the environmental and social impact of their suppliers. They implement rigorous sourcing standards, conduct audits, and collaborate with suppliers to improve sustainability performance. For example, brands sourcing raw materials like cotton, cocoa, or palm oil often work with certified suppliers, invest in local community development, and implement traceability systems to ensure ethical and sustainable practices throughout the value chain.

**Transparent communication and reporting** reinforce credibility. Brands leading sustainability do not rely on vague or superficial claims; they provide measurable, verifiable evidence of progress toward environmental and social goals. Sustainability reports, third-party certifications, and clear labeling educate consumers and demonstrate accountability. By openly sharing successes and challenges, these brands build trust with conscious consumers and investors who scrutinize authenticity and impact.

**Consumer engagement and education** are central to leadership. Sustainable brands actively involve consumers in their mission, encouraging responsible behavior, reuse, recycling, or participation in social initiatives. Campaigns often highlight practical steps consumers can take to reduce their environmental footprint while reinforcing the brand's purpose. This co-creation approach strengthens loyalty, advocacy, and alignment between brand values and consumer behavior.

**Collaboration and partnerships** amplify impact. Leading consumer brands often partner with NGOs, startups, government agencies, and industry consortia to address systemic sustainability challenges. By pooling resources, knowledge, and influence, brands can drive broader change across sectors, communities, and global supply chains. Collaborative initiatives may include renewable energy adoption, waste reduction programs, or social development projects, demonstrating a commitment beyond profit-driven objectives.

**Metrics and accountability** distinguish leaders from followers. These brands track ESG performance rigorously, using KPIs and analytics to measure progress on carbon reduction, water conservation, ethical sourcing, and social impact. Data-driven insights inform strategy, highlight areas for improvement, and ensure that sustainability efforts deliver tangible, verifiable results. Metrics also allow leaders to communicate impact effectively to stakeholders, reinforcing transparency and trust.

**Influence on industry standards** is a hallmark of leadership. Consumer brands at the forefront of sustainability often shape industry norms, inspiring competitors, regulators, and suppliers to elevate their practices. By setting ambitious goals and demonstrating feasibility, these brands create ripple effects that advance sustainability beyond their immediate operations. This leadership strengthens brand reputation while driving systemic change in markets, communities, and supply chains.

**Challenges in leading sustainability** include balancing cost, scalability, and performance, managing complex global supply chains, avoiding greenwashing, and navigating evolving regulations. Leading brands address these challenges through innovation, technology adoption, strategic partnerships, and stakeholder engagement. They view sustainability as a long-term investment rather than a short-term expense, ensuring alignment between ethical commitments and business growth.

Finally, **long-term brand equity and market differentiation** are reinforced by sustainability leadership. Conscious consumers, investors, and partners increasingly reward brands that demonstrate authentic, measurable commitment to environmental and social responsibility. Brands that successfully integrate sustainability into their operations, products, and communications build loyalty, advocacy, and resilience, positioning themselves as leaders in both purpose and profit.

# B2B and Industrial Sustainability Leaders

**B2B and Industrial Sustainability Leaders** explore how companies operating in business-to-business (B2B) and industrial sectors are integrating sustainability into operations, products, and client relationships. Unlike consumer-facing brands, B2B and industrial leaders focus on complex supply chains, large-scale production processes, and operational efficiency, making sustainability both a strategic necessity and a competitive differentiator. These leaders demonstrate that environmental stewardship, social responsibility, and ethical governance are not limited to consumer marketing but are critical drivers of innovation, operational resilience, and long-term business performance in industrial contexts.

At the core, **B2B and industrial sustainability leadership** is about embedding environmental, social, and governance (ESG) principles into every facet of operations, from procurement and manufacturing to logistics, energy consumption, and product lifecycle management. Industrial companies often have significant ecological footprints due to energy-intensive processes, chemical use, or raw material extraction. Leaders in this space adopt strategies to reduce emissions, minimize waste, optimize resource utilization, and implement circular economy practices, while ensuring compliance with evolving regulations and stakeholder expectations.

**Operational efficiency and decarbonization** are central to leadership in industrial sustainability. Companies invest in renewable energy, energy-efficient equipment, process optimization, and emissions reduction technologies to lower environmental impact. For example, manufacturing leaders may implement advanced energy management systems, adopt carbon capture solutions, or redesign processes to reduce waste and water consumption. These initiatives not only improve ESG performance but also generate cost savings, operational resilience, and regulatory compliance.

**Sustainable product innovation** distinguishes leaders in B2B markets. Industrial companies increasingly develop products and solutions that enable their clients to meet sustainability goals. This includes energy-efficient machinery, eco-friendly building materials, low-emission industrial equipment, and software solutions for monitoring environmental impact. By providing clients with tools to reduce their carbon footprint or enhance resource efficiency, these companies extend sustainability impact across the value chain while strengthening business relationships.

**Supply chain leadership** is a critical differentiator. Industrial sustainability leaders prioritize responsible sourcing, supplier audits, and transparency across multi-tiered supply chains. They collaborate with suppliers to improve environmental performance, reduce ethical risks, and ensure compliance with labor and safety standards. Advanced traceability and digital monitoring enable leaders to assess environmental impact, identify bottlenecks, and mitigate risks across global networks, reinforcing credibility and reliability for clients.

**Client engagement and co-creation** are key strategies. Industrial leaders work closely with B2B clients to co-develop sustainable solutions, provide ESG expertise, and align operational practices. By offering sustainability consulting, certification support, and transparent reporting, companies demonstrate value beyond the product itself. This approach strengthens partnerships, enhances loyalty, and positions the brand as a trusted advisor rather than just a supplier.

**Regulatory alignment and risk mitigation** are essential in industrial sectors. Leaders proactively monitor and comply with local and international regulations related to emissions, waste management, worker safety, and environmental reporting. Compliance reduces operational and reputational risks and ensures that sustainability practices are both legally sound and ethically responsible. Additionally, many industrial leaders adopt voluntary frameworks, such as ISO 14001 (environmental management) or Science-Based Targets, to exceed minimum compliance and demonstrate commitment to continuous improvement.

**Data-driven sustainability management** enables leaders to measure, optimize, and communicate performance. B2B and industrial companies utilize advanced analytics, IoT sensors, and digital twins to track energy use, emissions, and resource efficiency in real time. Insights from this data inform strategic decisions, process improvements, and client reporting, ensuring that sustainability goals are measurable, actionable, and transparent.

**Collaborations and industry leadership** further amplify impact. B2B sustainability leaders often participate in industry consortia, joint research initiatives, and public-private partnerships to address systemic environmental and social challenges. These collaborations accelerate innovation, standardize best practices, and influence sector-wide transformation, positioning the brand as a leader in both performance and purpose.

**Long-term business value and competitive advantage** are reinforced through sustainability leadership. Industrial companies that demonstrate operational efficiency, ESG compliance, and client-focused sustainability solutions differentiate themselves in highly competitive B2B markets. Conscious clients increasingly prioritize suppliers who provide measurable impact, transparency, and alignment with their own sustainability commitments, rewarding leaders with stronger relationships and growth opportunities.

## Startups Disrupting Through Purpose

**Startups Disrupting Through Purpose** explores how new, agile companies are redefining markets by embedding sustainability, social responsibility, and ethical purpose at the core of their business models. Unlike traditional companies that may retrofit sustainability into existing operations, purpose-driven startups leverage their flexibility, innovation, and mission-oriented culture to create products, services, and business practices that address environmental and social challenges while capturing market opportunities. These startups demonstrate that purpose can be a powerful driver of differentiation, growth, and long-term brand equity.

At the core, **purpose-driven startups align business goals with societal impact**. Their mission is not only to generate profits but also to create positive change in the world. This alignment shapes product development, operations, marketing, and partnerships. For example, a startup may focus on producing biodegradable packaging, developing renewable energy solutions, or providing financial services to underserved communities. By embedding purpose from inception, these companies cultivate authenticity and credibility, attracting conscious consumers, investors, and partners.

**Innovation as a differentiator** is a defining characteristic of these startups. Purpose-driven startups often disrupt traditional industries by developing new technologies, business models, or delivery mechanisms that address environmental or social challenges. For instance, clean energy startups challenge fossil fuel dependence with scalable renewable solutions, while circular economy startups transform waste into valuable products. Innovation allows these companies to solve unmet needs while creating measurable sustainability outcomes, establishing themselves as leaders in emerging markets.

**Mission-driven branding and marketing** amplify the impact of purpose. Startups communicate their values and commitments clearly to consumers, investors, and partners, differentiating themselves in competitive markets. Authentic storytelling about social or environmental impact builds trust and loyalty among conscious consumers who seek meaningful connections with the brands they support. Purpose-driven messaging reinforces the company's identity and creates a compelling narrative that resonates across digital and physical touchpoints.

**Agility and responsiveness** enable startups to capitalize on emerging trends and shifting consumer expectations. Small, nimble teams can iterate quickly, test new ideas, and respond to feedback in ways that larger, established companies may struggle to match. This responsiveness allows startups to refine sustainable products, scale impactful initiatives, and adapt messaging to evolving market conditions without compromising their core purpose.

**Investor attraction and funding opportunities** are increasingly tied to purpose. Venture capitalists and impact investors are prioritizing startups that demonstrate both growth potential and measurable ESG outcomes. Purpose-driven startups can secure funding by showcasing innovative solutions to environmental or social problems, backed by data-driven impact metrics. This investment further enables them to scale operations, enhance R&D, and expand market reach while staying true to their mission.

**Collaborations and ecosystem engagement** are essential for scaling impact. Purpose-driven startups often partner with NGOs, industry consortia, academic institutions, or government agencies to accelerate innovation, gain credibility, and access resources. Co-creation with conscious consumers or stakeholders ensures that products and services are relevant, culturally sensitive, and effective. Such partnerships amplify the startup's reach and reinforce its commitment to sustainability and social responsibility.

**Measuring and communicating impact** is a critical success factor. Purpose-driven startups rigorously track ESG metrics, such as carbon reduction, resource efficiency, social inclusion, or community benefit, to validate claims and attract stakeholders. Transparent reporting, often through digital dashboards, social media, or sustainability reports, builds trust and accountability, differentiating the startup from competitors and signaling long-term commitment.

**Challenges in purpose-driven disruption** include balancing profitability with impact, navigating regulatory landscapes, managing resource constraints, and scaling operations sustainably. Startups must innovate business models that generate revenue while delivering measurable social or environmental value. Strategic planning, partnerships, and technology adoption are key to overcoming these challenges while maintaining mission alignment.

Finally, **long-term brand equity and market influence** are reinforced through purpose. Startups that successfully integrate mission-driven strategies build loyal customer bases, attract like-minded employees, and influence industry standards. Their disruptive approach not only addresses societal challenges but also inspires broader adoption of sustainable practices across industries, creating ripple effects that extend beyond immediate business outcomes.

## Lessons from Failures and Backlash

**Lessons from Failures and Backlash** explore the critical insights brands gain when sustainability initiatives, purpose-driven campaigns, or ethical commitments fall short of expectations. In a conscious consumer world, transparency and accountability mean that missteps are visible and can quickly erode trust, damage reputation, and reduce loyalty. While failures and backlash are challenging, they provide invaluable lessons that help organizations refine strategies, strengthen governance, and ultimately become more authentic, resilient, and effective in driving sustainable impact.

At the core, **failure often stems from a disconnect between intention and execution**. Brands may communicate sustainability commitments without implementing tangible actions, exaggerate claims, or misinterpret consumer priorities. When these inconsistencies are exposed, stakeholders perceive greenwashing or hypocrisy, leading to public backlash. For example, a company that markets a product as "eco-friendly" but relies on suppliers with poor environmental or labor practices risks reputational damage, negative media coverage, and consumer boycotts. Such failures underscore the importance of aligning purpose, strategy, and operations coherently.

**Lack of transparency and accountability** is another common cause of backlash. Brands that fail to provide measurable, verifiable evidence for their sustainability claims leave themselves vulnerable to skepticism and criticism. Conscious consumers and watchdog organizations increasingly demand data-backed proof, third-party certifications, and open reporting. Failing to meet these expectations can result in reputational damage and erosion of trust, highlighting the need for rigorous monitoring, reporting, and validation of all claims.

**Misalignment with consumer values or cultural context** often triggers backlash. A campaign or initiative that resonates in one market may be misunderstood, irrelevant, or offensive in another. Cultural insensitivity, poor localization, or overgeneralized messaging can alienate audiences and provoke negative attention. Lessons from such failures emphasize the importance of thorough cultural research, stakeholder engagement, and sensitivity in communication strategies.

**Overpromising or underdelivering** is a key pitfall. Brands that set ambitious sustainability goals without clear implementation plans risk disappointing stakeholders when targets are not met. This can result in criticism from consumers, investors, and media, undermining credibility. Effective lesson-taking requires brands to balance ambition with realism, set measurable milestones, and communicate progress honestly, demonstrating accountability even when challenges arise.

**Internal misalignment and governance gaps** contribute to failure. Sustainability initiatives often fail when they are isolated within marketing teams without engagement from operations, supply chain, or leadership. Lack of cross-functional coordination can lead to inconsistencies, operational inefficiencies, or unfulfilled commitments. Lessons learned emphasize integrating sustainability into the core business strategy, ensuring that all departments share ownership of purpose-driven goals.

**Backlash provides opportunities for learning and improvement**. Brands can use public scrutiny as a catalyst to refine processes, strengthen policies, and enhance transparency. For example, companies facing criticism for supply chain labor practices may implement stricter audits, supplier training programs, and reporting mechanisms. By responding proactively, brands demonstrate accountability, resilience, and a willingness to improve, which can restore trust and even strengthen consumer loyalty over time.

**Effective crisis management** is essential when failures occur. Brands must respond quickly, openly, and authentically, acknowledging shortcomings, explaining corrective actions, and committing to continuous improvement. Silence, defensiveness, or vague messaging can exacerbate backlash, while clear, evidence-backed responses help mitigate reputational harm and signal genuine accountability.

**Stakeholder engagement and co-creation** are critical lessons from backlash. Involving consumers, employees, partners, and community stakeholders in designing, implementing, and refining sustainability initiatives reduces the risk of misalignment and enhances relevance. Feedback loops provide early warning signs, enable course corrections, and demonstrate that the brand values stakeholder perspectives.

**Continuous learning and adaptation** are central to long-term resilience. Failure is not inherently negative if brands treat it as an opportunity for reflection, course correction, and strategy refinement. Lessons from missteps should inform governance, reporting, supply chain practices, communication strategies, and product development, ensuring that future initiatives are more robust, authentic, and impactful.

Finally, **maintaining credibility and long-term brand equity** depends on how failures and backlash are managed. Brands that demonstrate transparency, accountability, cultural awareness, and responsiveness can recover from setbacks while strengthening stakeholder trust. Conversely, repeated missteps or lack of corrective action can erode reputation, reduce consumer loyalty, and undermine the effectiveness of future sustainability initiatives.

## Key Takeaways and Replicable Models

**Key Takeaways and Replicable Models** focus on synthesizing the insights, strategies, and best practices that emerge from successful sustainability initiatives, purpose-driven campaigns, and brand leadership in a conscious consumer world. This sub-chapter provides a framework for businesses to translate learning into actionable strategies that can be adapted, scaled, and replicated across markets, industries, and organizational contexts. By codifying what works, organizations can accelerate impact, avoid common pitfalls, and embed sustainability into core operations without compromising authenticity or brand values.

At the core, **key takeaways summarize lessons learned from diverse sustainability efforts**. These include the importance of aligning purpose with operations, embedding ESG principles into decision-making, leveraging data for strategic action, engaging stakeholders meaningfully, and maintaining cultural sensitivity. Other critical insights emphasize transparency, accountability, and long-term thinking, highlighting that sustainability is not a short-term marketing tactic but a continuous, integrated approach that enhances credibility, consumer trust, and business resilience.

**Replicable models** refer to structured approaches, frameworks, and processes that can be adapted across contexts to achieve sustainability and purpose-driven outcomes. Examples include circular economy practices, ethical supply chain management, sustainable product innovation, stakeholder engagement frameworks, and purpose-driven marketing strategies. By documenting these models, organizations create blueprints that reduce uncertainty, standardize best practices, and enable teams to implement initiatives consistently while allowing for local adaptation.

**Strategic integration** is a key component of replicable models. Leading brands demonstrate that sustainability is most effective when embedded in core business strategy rather than isolated initiatives. This includes aligning mission, vision, and values with operational goals, incorporating ESG metrics into performance evaluations, and ensuring that every department—from R&D and operations to marketing and sales—supports sustainability objectives. A replicable model therefore includes governance structures, decision-making processes, and cross-functional collaboration mechanisms that can be applied across projects and geographies.

**Data-driven decision-making** is another critical element. Replicable models incorporate robust measurement systems, key performance indicators (KPIs), and reporting frameworks that allow organizations to track progress, assess impact, and inform continuous improvement. By using standardized metrics, brands can replicate successful strategies, compare outcomes across markets, and identify areas for optimization. Data also supports transparency, enabling stakeholders to understand and trust the brand's sustainability efforts.

**Stakeholder engagement frameworks** provide replicable guidance on involving consumers, employees, suppliers, NGOs, and investors in sustainability initiatives. Structured approaches to co-creation, feedback loops, and participatory design ensure that initiatives are relevant, culturally sensitive, and impactful. This approach not only reduces the risk of backlash but also fosters advocacy, loyalty, and collective ownership of sustainability outcomes.

**Innovation and agility** are central to replicable models. Effective frameworks emphasize iterative testing, piloting, and scaling of sustainability initiatives. Startups and established brands alike benefit from approaches that allow experimentation while embedding lessons learned into standardized practices. Agile models encourage responsiveness to market trends, regulatory changes, and evolving consumer expectations without compromising core brand values.

**Communication and storytelling strategies** are another replicable component. Leading brands use structured approaches to convey sustainability initiatives authentically, integrating visual, digital, and experiential channels to reach diverse audiences. Key elements include clear articulation of purpose, evidence-backed claims, local adaptation, and engagement-focused narratives. Replicating these strategies across campaigns ensures consistency, credibility, and resonance.

**Risk management and compliance mechanisms** are essential to sustaining replicable models. Processes that proactively assess legal, ethical, and reputational risks ensure that sustainability initiatives are resilient and adaptable. These mechanisms allow brands to anticipate challenges, maintain regulatory alignment, and prevent negative outcomes, reinforcing trust and long-term credibility.

**Lessons learned from failures** are equally important in creating replicable models. By analyzing setbacks, misalignments, and backlash, organizations can refine frameworks, improve processes, and build safeguards into future initiatives. Incorporating these insights ensures that models are robust, practical, and resilient under diverse operational and cultural conditions.

Finally, **scalability and adaptability** are fundamental to replicable models. Successful frameworks are designed to be flexible enough to accommodate local market nuances, cultural differences, and operational constraints while maintaining alignment with core sustainability and purpose-driven principles. This balance allows organizations to extend impact globally without diluting values or compromising authenticity.

# The Future of Sustainable Marketing

# Climate Change and Marketing Accountability

**Climate Change and Marketing Accountability** examines the responsibility of brands to address climate-related challenges through their operations, products, and communications while ensuring transparency, honesty, and measurable impact. In an era where consumers, regulators, and investors increasingly demand climate-conscious behavior, marketing plays a central role in conveying a brand's sustainability commitments. However, claims about carbon reduction, renewable energy use, or climate-positive products must be credible, data-backed, and aligned with actual business practices to maintain trust and avoid accusations of greenwashing.

At its core, **marketing accountability for climate change** involves ensuring that all communications reflect genuine actions and measurable outcomes. Brands must avoid overstating achievements or making ambiguous claims, as these can erode consumer confidence and invite scrutiny from watchdogs, regulators, or media. For instance, stating that a product is "eco-friendly" without quantifying carbon reduction or demonstrating lifecycle sustainability risks backlash. Accountability requires integrating marketing with operational transparency, reporting frameworks, and verifiable data.

**Transparency in sustainability claims** is essential. Marketing teams must clearly communicate the scope, methodology, and outcomes of climate initiatives. This may include providing information about carbon footprint, renewable energy sourcing, emissions reduction strategies, or offsets. Third-party certifications, independent audits, and clear labeling reinforce credibility and allow consumers to make informed decisions. Transparent marketing fosters trust, demonstrates integrity, and differentiates brands in competitive markets.

**Alignment with corporate strategy and operations** is a critical component. Climate-related marketing claims must reflect real actions across supply chains, production processes, and product design. For example, promoting a carbon-neutral product requires tangible steps such as energy-efficient manufacturing, sustainable sourcing, and verified carbon offset programs. Marketing accountability ensures that promotional messages are not isolated from operational reality, bridging purpose with practice.

**Regulatory compliance and industry standards** guide accountable climate marketing. Laws, guidelines, and frameworks—such as the Federal Trade Commission's Green Guides in the U.S., ISO standards, or EU environmental directives—set expectations for truthful environmental claims. Brands must adhere to these requirements to avoid legal consequences and reinforce credibility with conscious consumers and investors. Understanding and applying regulatory guidance ensures that climate messaging meets both legal and ethical standards.

**Data-driven communication** enhances accountability. Marketing teams should leverage analytics, sustainability dashboards, and impact reporting to substantiate claims. Quantifiable metrics—such as carbon reductions, renewable energy usage, water conservation, or waste diversion—provide evidence that supports marketing narratives. Using accurate data reduces the risk of exaggeration, improves credibility, and allows brands to track progress over time.

**Consumer education and engagement** are important dimensions of accountable marketing. Beyond promoting products, brands have an opportunity to inform consumers about climate challenges, sustainable practices, and responsible consumption. Educational campaigns that empower audiences to reduce their carbon footprint or participate in sustainability initiatives amplify brand impact while reinforcing authenticity. Accountability entails not just messaging but also fostering informed action among stakeholders.

**Managing risk and mitigating greenwashing** is a critical responsibility. Misleading climate claims can provoke public backlash, negative media coverage, and reputational damage. Brands must proactively evaluate messaging, validate claims, and implement internal review processes to prevent inaccuracies. Lessons from prior failures in sustainability marketing highlight the importance of oversight, ethical review, and alignment between marketing and operational realities.

**Collaboration and partnerships** reinforce accountability. Engaging with NGOs, certification bodies, industry consortia, and government programs helps validate initiatives and ensures that climate messaging is credible and consistent. Third-party verification adds authority to claims and demonstrates a commitment to rigorous standards beyond self-reporting.

**Long-term brand trust and competitive advantage** are strengthened through accountable climate marketing. Consumers increasingly reward brands that communicate honestly, demonstrate measurable impact, and take meaningful action on climate change. Authentic marketing not only drives loyalty and advocacy but also positions the brand as a leader in sustainability, attracting conscious consumers, investors, and partners.

## Policy, Regulation, and Industry Standards

**Policy, Regulation, and Industry Standards** examine the frameworks that guide businesses in implementing sustainability, ethical practices, and responsible marketing. In a conscious consumer world, brands operate under increasing scrutiny from governments, industry bodies, and civil society, making adherence to policies, regulations, and standards essential for credibility, operational integrity, and competitive advantage. Understanding these frameworks enables companies to navigate legal obligations, benchmark performance, and align strategies with best practices across environmental, social, and governance (ESG) domains.

At the core, **policy frameworks** refer to governmental or intergovernmental rules that dictate how businesses should operate in relation to environmental protection, labor standards, product safety, and corporate governance. Policies may include emission limits, renewable energy mandates, waste management directives, or labor protections. Compliance ensures that businesses operate legally, mitigate risk, and contribute to societal and environmental goals. Policies also provide the foundation for corporate sustainability strategies, informing operational decisions, reporting practices, and stakeholder engagement.

**Regulations** are legally enforceable requirements established by governmental authorities. Unlike voluntary policies or guidelines, regulations carry consequences for non-compliance, including fines, sanctions, or reputational harm. For example, the European Union's Corporate Sustainability Reporting Directive (CSRD) mandates detailed ESG disclosures for large companies, while the U.S. Environmental Protection Agency sets enforceable emissions standards. Regulations create accountability and push companies to integrate sustainable practices into their core operations, product design, and supply chain management.

**Industry standards** represent voluntary or semi-mandatory benchmarks established by trade associations, professional bodies, or international organizations. Standards provide consistent methodologies, best practices, and performance metrics for companies to follow. Examples include ISO 14001 for environmental management systems, ISO 45001 for occupational health and safety, and ISO 26000 for social responsibility. Industry standards help companies benchmark performance, demonstrate compliance, and signal credibility to stakeholders, particularly in B2B markets or regulated industries.

**Alignment with policies and regulations** is critical for operational integrity and reputation management. Sustainable brands integrate regulatory requirements into strategy, ensuring that product design, supply chains, marketing claims, and corporate governance meet legal expectations. This proactive approach reduces risk, enhances stakeholder trust, and positions the company as a responsible actor in its sector. Compliance also enables smoother market entry across regions with varying legal frameworks, supporting global growth and scalability.

**Benchmarking and adoption of industry standards** create replicable frameworks for performance and accountability. Companies can leverage standards to set internal KPIs, monitor progress, and validate sustainability initiatives. For example, adherence to ISO 14001 may involve systematic environmental audits, resource efficiency programs, and continuous improvement cycles, which can then be reported transparently to consumers, investors, and regulatory bodies. Standards provide credibility and comparability, which are particularly valuable in industries where sustainability claims are heavily scrutinized.

**Stakeholder engagement and reporting** are enhanced through policy and standard adherence. Transparent communication about compliance with regulations and alignment with industry standards signals accountability to investors, consumers, employees, and partners. Sustainability reports, ESG disclosures, and third-party certifications demonstrate that a company is not only meeting legal requirements but also actively pursuing best practices and continuous improvement.

**Global and regional complexity** adds another layer of importance. Companies operating in multiple geographies must navigate diverse regulatory landscapes, differing environmental standards, and regional labor laws. Effective strategy involves harmonizing compliance across markets while respecting local policies and cultural contexts. Industry standards and certifications can serve as unifying frameworks, providing consistency and credibility even in diverse regulatory environments.

**Continuous monitoring and adaptation** are essential. Policies, regulations, and standards evolve as societal expectations, technological advances, and environmental imperatives change. Leading brands maintain mechanisms to track regulatory updates, participate in industry consultations, and adjust internal processes to remain compliant and competitive. This dynamic approach ensures resilience, reduces legal and reputational risk, and demonstrates leadership in sustainability.

**Integration into business strategy** ensures that compliance is not just a checkbox but a driver of long-term value. Companies that embed regulatory and standards compliance into innovation, marketing, supply chain management, and stakeholder engagement gain operational efficiency, enhance brand trust, and unlock competitive advantages. Policy and standard adherence becomes both a safeguard and a growth enabler, aligning legal, ethical, and commercial objectives.

## Technology's Role in Sustainable Growth

**Technology's Role in Sustainable Growth** explores how digital innovation, advanced tools, and emerging technologies drive efficiency, transparency, and scalability in sustainability initiatives. In a conscious consumer world, technology enables companies to integrate environmental, social, and governance (ESG) principles into operations, products, and marketing strategies while generating measurable impact. From resource optimization to data-driven decision-making, technology acts as a critical enabler of sustainable growth, allowing businesses to achieve both purpose and profitability simultaneously.

At the core, **technology enhances operational efficiency**, reducing resource consumption, emissions, and waste across the value chain. Advanced manufacturing systems, automation, and Internet of Things (IoT) sensors monitor energy use, water consumption, and material efficiency in real time. Predictive analytics can optimize production schedules, logistics routes, and inventory management, minimizing environmental impact while lowering operational costs. By leveraging these tools, companies can scale sustainable practices without compromising performance or profitability.

**Data analytics and monitoring platforms** are central to measuring, managing, and improving sustainability performance. Businesses can track carbon emissions, water usage, waste generation, and supply chain compliance with unprecedented accuracy. Advanced dashboards, digital twins, and AI-driven insights enable proactive identification of inefficiencies, benchmarking against industry standards, and reporting to stakeholders. Data-driven approaches ensure that sustainability initiatives are measurable, verifiable, and aligned with both regulatory requirements and corporate goals.

**Supply chain transparency and traceability** are significantly enhanced through technology. Blockchain, RFID tracking, and cloud-based platforms allow companies to trace materials, verify supplier compliance, and ensure ethical sourcing across complex global networks. Transparency not only mitigates risk and prevents greenwashing but also strengthens credibility with conscious consumers, investors, and partners. These technologies create end-to-end visibility, enabling companies to respond quickly to disruptions while maintaining ESG standards.

**Sustainable product innovation** benefits from technological advancements. Materials science, renewable energy solutions, biodegradable packaging, and energy-efficient designs are increasingly powered by research, simulation, and digital prototyping tools. Startups and established companies alike leverage technology to create products with lower environmental footprints, optimized performance, and longer lifecycles. This intersection of innovation and sustainability differentiates brands in competitive markets and meets growing consumer demand for responsible products.

**Digital marketing and communication technologies** play a key role in conveying sustainability initiatives authentically. Tools for personalized messaging, interactive content, and data-backed storytelling enable brands to demonstrate impact transparently and engage conscious consumers effectively. AI and analytics help refine campaigns, measure engagement, and optimize messaging for relevance and credibility, ensuring that sustainability claims resonate without exaggeration or ambiguity.

**Energy management and renewable technologies** are central to sustainable growth. Smart grids, energy storage, solar and wind technologies, and AI-driven energy optimization systems allow companies to reduce carbon footprints, improve operational resilience, and achieve climate-related goals. These technologies enable companies to integrate sustainability into core operations rather than treating it as a peripheral initiative, demonstrating genuine commitment to environmental responsibility.

**Collaboration and innovation ecosystems** are facilitated by technology. Digital platforms connect businesses with NGOs, startups, research institutions, and government bodies to co-create sustainable solutions. Open innovation networks and collaborative tools accelerate problem-solving, knowledge sharing, and scalable solutions to complex sustainability challenges. Technology thus enables collective action, amplifying impact beyond individual organizational boundaries.

**Consumer engagement and behavior change** can be influenced through technology-driven solutions. Mobile apps, gamified platforms, and IoT-enabled products allow consumers to monitor energy use, waste reduction, or responsible consumption patterns. By integrating sustainability into user experiences, technology empowers conscious choices and fosters loyalty while reinforcing the brand's purpose-driven narrative.

**Regulatory compliance and reporting** are simplified through technology. Automated reporting tools, ESG dashboards, and compliance software ensure that companies meet local and global requirements efficiently. This reduces administrative burden, minimizes errors, and enhances transparency, allowing organizations to focus on strategic sustainability initiatives while demonstrating accountability to stakeholders.

Finally, **technology as a driver of long-term sustainable growth** enables organizations to balance economic performance with environmental and social responsibility. Companies that effectively harness technology can innovate, scale, and optimize sustainably, reinforcing brand credibility, enhancing consumer trust, and achieving measurable impact. Technology transforms sustainability from a tactical consideration into a strategic growth driver, positioning brands to succeed in a conscious, evolving marketplace.

# From Conscious Consumers to Conscious Systems

**From Conscious Consumers to Conscious Systems** explores the evolution of sustainability thinking from individual consumer choices to holistic, systemic approaches that embed responsibility across entire industries, supply chains, and societal structures. While early sustainability efforts focused primarily on influencing consumer behavior—encouraging eco-friendly purchases, ethical consumption, and responsible lifestyles—the next frontier involves creating interconnected systems that inherently support environmental, social, and governance (ESG) objectives. This shift recognizes that true sustainable impact requires structural change, not just individual action.

At its core, **conscious consumers drive the initial momentum for sustainability**. Awareness of environmental degradation, social inequities, and ethical issues has led individuals to prefer brands that reflect their values. Consumers increasingly demand transparency, ethical sourcing, climate accountability, and products with minimal environmental impact. This pressure motivates companies to adapt, innovate, and communicate sustainability initiatives, creating a market incentive for responsible behavior. Conscious consumerism catalyzes change by signaling the demand for responsible products and ethical business practices.

**Conscious systems**, however, extend the responsibility beyond the individual consumer to include corporations, governments, regulators, industry consortia, and technology platforms. These systems recognize that individual behavior alone cannot address complex sustainability challenges such as climate change, deforestation, or labor inequities. For example, a consumer may choose a sustainable product, but if the production process relies on unsustainable supply chains, the net impact is limited. Designing systemic solutions ensures that sustainability is integrated into every stage of production, distribution, and consumption.

**Supply chain and operational systems** exemplify conscious systems in practice. Leading companies are moving toward circular economy models, ethical sourcing, and regenerative practices that reduce environmental impact while creating social value. By embedding sustainability into supplier contracts, logistics optimization, and manufacturing practices, companies create a framework where every stakeholder contributes to positive outcomes. Technology, such as blockchain, IoT monitoring, and data analytics, enables visibility and accountability across these systems, ensuring that responsibility is shared and enforced at scale.

**Policy and regulatory systems** are another key component. Governments and industry bodies increasingly establish rules, incentives, and standards that promote sustainability at an ecosystem level. Regulations on emissions, labor practices, and ESG reporting, alongside industry certifications and voluntary frameworks, create structures that compel companies to align with broader societal goals. By combining consumer demand with systemic policy enforcement, sustainability becomes embedded into market mechanisms rather than dependent solely on individual choice.

**Technology and digital platforms** facilitate the transition from consumer-focused approaches to system-level solutions. Platforms that enable energy management, waste tracking, supply chain transparency, and sustainable financing allow stakeholders to make interconnected, informed decisions. Artificial intelligence and predictive analytics can model environmental impact, optimize resource allocation, and support scalable climate-positive initiatives. Technology transforms isolated efforts into integrated systems where sustainability outcomes are measurable, repeatable, and continuously improving.

**Collaborative ecosystems** reinforce conscious systems. Companies, NGOs, governments, and communities collaborate to address systemic challenges that no single actor could solve alone. Partnerships on renewable energy adoption, water stewardship, ethical labor practices, and circular materials create collective impact, magnifying the effectiveness of sustainability initiatives. Conscious systems foster co-creation, shared responsibility, and accountability across stakeholders, ensuring that positive change is sustainable and scalable.

**Shifting metrics and incentives** are also critical. Traditional business success metrics, such as profit and growth, are being supplemented with system-level sustainability KPIs: carbon reduction, resource efficiency, community development, and ESG alignment. By embedding these metrics into governance, supply chains, and decision-making, organizations ensure that systemic outcomes are prioritized alongside financial performance.

**Education and culture** underpin conscious systems. Consumers, employees, and partners must understand systemic impact, interdependencies, and collective responsibility. Awareness programs, training, and transparent communication help stakeholders recognize their role within broader sustainable systems, reinforcing behavior that supports systemic objectives rather than isolated actions.

Finally, **long-term impact and resilience** are maximized through conscious systems. While conscious consumers catalyze demand, systemic integration ensures that sustainability is embedded structurally, mitigating risk, enhancing operational efficiency, and enabling scalable change. Brands that contribute to and operate within conscious systems build enduring trust, credibility, and competitive advantage while driving measurable environmental and social outcomes.

## Preparing Brands for the Next Decade

**Preparing Brands for the Next Decade** explores the strategies, mindsets, and structural adaptations that companies must adopt to remain competitive, relevant, and purpose-driven in an increasingly conscious, fast-evolving global marketplace. The next decade will be defined by heightened consumer awareness, rapid technological change, tightening regulatory landscapes, and urgent environmental and social challenges. Brands that anticipate these shifts and embed sustainability, purpose, and innovation at their core will not only survive but thrive, building long-term resilience and competitive advantage.

At the core, **future-ready brands embrace purpose as a strategic imperative**. Purpose is no longer a peripheral marketing message—it is a guiding principle for decision-making, product innovation, and organizational culture. Brands that clearly define and authentically execute their mission, aligned with consumer values and societal needs, are better positioned to attract loyal customers, engaged employees, and supportive investors. Purpose-driven strategies serve as a compass for navigating complex challenges while differentiating brands in crowded markets.

**Sustainability integration** will be essential. The next decade will demand that environmental, social, and governance (ESG) considerations are embedded into every aspect of the business, from supply chains and manufacturing processes to marketing, product design, and customer engagement. Companies must commit to measurable impact, including carbon reduction, circular economy adoption, responsible sourcing, and ethical labor practices. By making sustainability operational rather than symbolic, brands align themselves with both regulatory trends and the expectations of conscious consumers.

**Technological innovation and digital transformation** are critical enablers. Future-ready brands leverage artificial intelligence, automation, big data, IoT, and advanced analytics to optimize operations, reduce environmental impact, and engage consumers meaningfully. Digital tools allow brands to track ESG performance, improve supply chain transparency, predict consumer trends, and deliver personalized, responsible experiences. Integrating technology into sustainability strategies enables scalability, efficiency, and responsiveness to market changes.

**Agility and adaptability** will define competitive resilience. The next decade will bring unpredictable disruptions, from geopolitical shifts and economic volatility to climate crises and social movements. Brands that foster flexible organizational structures, iterative product development, and responsive marketing can adapt quickly while maintaining alignment with purpose and values. Agility ensures that brands remain relevant, seize emerging opportunities, and mitigate risks in complex environments.

**Consumer engagement and co-creation** will be increasingly important. Brands must move beyond one-way communication to involve customers, communities, and stakeholders in shaping products, services, and initiatives. Co-creation strengthens loyalty, ensures relevance, and fosters collective responsibility for sustainability outcomes. Conscious consumers will favor brands that actively demonstrate transparency, inclusivity, and meaningful impact.

**Employee engagement and internal culture** are equally critical. Organizations must cultivate cultures that value sustainability, innovation, and ethical decision-making. Employees are brand ambassadors, and their advocacy is crucial for purpose-driven marketing, product development, and operations. Investing in training, empowerment, and recognition ensures that internal teams can execute on ambitious sustainability and purpose initiatives effectively.

**Collaboration and ecosystem thinking** will amplify impact. Future-ready brands will increasingly partner with startups, NGOs, governments, and other industry players to tackle systemic challenges such as climate change, social inequality, and resource scarcity. Collaborative approaches create shared value, accelerate innovation, and establish brands as leaders in sustainable and ethical business practices.

**Data-driven accountability and measurement** will underpin credibility. Brands must implement robust ESG metrics, monitoring systems, and reporting frameworks to demonstrate tangible impact. Transparent reporting, third-party verification, and clear communication of outcomes reinforce trust with consumers, investors, and regulators, while also enabling continuous improvement.

**Regulatory foresight** is a critical consideration. With sustainability and ethical practices moving to the center of policy agendas globally, brands must anticipate evolving regulations, adapt strategies proactively, and ensure compliance across markets. Forward-looking governance allows companies to minimize risk, avoid penalties, and capitalize on incentives while reinforcing credibility and stakeholder confidence.

Finally, **long-term brand resilience and differentiation** will stem from the ability to integrate purpose, sustainability, innovation, and operational excellence seamlessly. Brands that prepare strategically for the next decade position themselves not only to respond to emerging challenges but also to shape industry standards, influence consumer behavior, and create lasting social and environmental impact.

Dear **Readers**,

Thank you for taking the time to explore *Sustainable Marketing: Winning in a Conscious Consumer World*. Your commitment to understanding the evolving landscape of purpose-driven branding, sustainability, and conscious business practices is a testament to the change our world needs.

This book was written with the hope of providing actionable insights, inspiring strategies, and a roadmap for integrating sustainability into every facet of marketing and business. By reading it, you are joining a growing community of leaders, marketers, and innovators who recognize that meaningful impact and business success are not mutually exclusive—they are deeply interconnected.

As you move forward, I hope the ideas, case studies, and frameworks shared here empower you to create authentic, responsible, and future-ready brands. May your actions inspire conscious choices, foster lasting trust with stakeholders, and contribute to a world where purpose, sustainability, and growth thrive together.

Thank you for your curiosity, your commitment, and your willingness to lead with conscience. The journey toward sustainable marketing is ongoing, and your role as a conscious changemaker makes all the difference.

**Divyam Agarwal**
Author, "Sustainable Marketing"

# More Books by the Author

The Author, Divyam has published numerous comprehensive guides aimed at helping individuals and organizations navigate the complex world of digital marketing, branding, and web development. His notable works include:

- Agarwal, Divyam (1 January 2024) "Digital Dynamo: Navigating the Landscape of Digital Marketing" Self-Published (English) ISBN: 978-93-6123-996-0
- Agarwal, Divyam (15 January 2024) "Mastering SEO: A Comprehensive Guide to Dominating Search Engines" Self-Published (English) ISBN: 978-93-6128-989-7
- Agarwal, Divyam (31 January 2024) "Mobile Mastery: A Comprehensive Guide to Dominating the Mobile Marketing Landscape" Self-Published (English) ISBN: 978-93-340-0427-4
- Agarwal, Divyam (1 February 2024) "Social Symphony: A Comprehensive Guide to Mastering Social Media Marketing" Self-Published (English) ISBN: 978-93-6128-219-5
- Agarwal, Divyam (15 February 2024) "Automate to Captivate: A Comprehensive Guide to Marketing Automation" Self-Published (English) ISBN: 978-93-340-0570-7
- Agarwal, Divyam (29 February 2024) "The Art and Science of Advertising: Mastering the Marketing Game" Self-Published (English) ISBN: 978-93-340-0927-9
- Agarwal, Divyam (1 March 2024) "Brand You: Mastering the Art of Personal Branding and Press Releases" Self-Published (English) ISBN: 978-93-6128-418-2
- Agarwal, Divyam (15 March 2024) "Web Mastery: A Comprehensive Guide to Modern Web Development and Design" Self-Published (English) ISBN: 978-93-340-1361-0
- Agarwal, Divyam (1 April 2024) "The Influencer Code: Mastering the Art and Science of Influencer Marketing" Self-Published (English) ISBN: 978-93-6128-565-3
- Agarwal, Divyam (1 June 2024) "Omnichannel Marketing: Bridging the Gap Between Online and Offline Experiences" Self-Published (English) ISBN: 978-93-340-9587-6

www.ingramcontent.com/pod-product-compliance
Lightning Source LLC
Chambersburg PA
CBHW050526240926
51846CB00003B/706
* 9 7 8 9 3 3 4 2 9 6 7 2 3 *